GOD COMES TO NASHVILLE
SPOTLIGHTS ON MUSIC CITY PERSONALITIES

GOD COMES TO NASHVILLE
SPOTLIGHTS ON MUSIC CITY PERSONALITIES

by Darryl E. Hicks

New Leaf Press
P.O. BOX 1045, HARRISON, ARK. 72601

First Edition, 1979

Cover design: Peter Hope

Typesetting: *Type-O-Graphics*

Library of Congress Catalog Number: 79-89583

International Standard Book Number: 0-89221-065-6

CONTENTS

DEDICATION

This book is lovingly dedicated to four of the most beautiful parents two people could have:

    Mabel S. Hicks
    Gifford R. Hicks
    Mary N. Allebach
    Harold M. Allebach

Also, a special thanks to my wife, Karen, for her help, support, proofreading, and love.

FOREWORD

As I boarded an airplane from Nashville to Los Angeles, California, I was extremely tired from the full schedule I had during the previous week. I thought: *How nice . . . the flight is four hours long so I'll have a chance to catch up on my sleep.* I buckled myself in and rested my head back. Then the stewardess announced breakfast would be served when we were in the air. Since I was hungry, I thought, *Oh, well, I'll just read some of this manuscript until breakfast comes.*

I've read and heard so much about the Nashville scene, as I unwrapped the manuscript I hoped I might find something new in this. Boy, was I in for a surprise! The very first chapter caught my attention. I was naturally curious about John Brown, the convicted killer of Stringbean. I had known Stringbean for years and had worked shows with him when I was in show business. The story and the detailed facts about John Brown were so interesting. I just kept on reading . . . until I had read most of the manuscript before we landed.

I feel this book is a fresh approach to the Nashville scene. It is well written and very informative, and I believe it will be a great inspiration and tool of the Lord to encourage some friend or loved one to surrender to Jesus Christ. You'll want to read it and pass it on. Matthew 16:26.

--Jimmy Snow, D.D., Th.B.

PREFACE

Not long ago while in Nashvile working on another book, Marijohn Wilkin took me to a prayer fellowship one afternoon. It had already started when we arrived, so when we found two empty chairs, I looked around to those in the room. The faces looked familiar. I turned to Marijohn with a question mark on my face. She leaned over and began whispering the names that fit the faces. It was like a music "Who's Who!"

Teddy Wilburn of the Wilburn Brothers—Grand Ole Opry was singing a song about the difference God had made in his life. The pretty blonde sitting opposite us listened intently to the words; her name—Skeeter Davis ("Last Date" and "The End of the World"). Billy Walker ("Charlie's Shoes") sat over in the corner with a special peace and smile etched on his face. Right next to my chair, Jeannie C. Riley ("Harper Valley PTA") held a leather-bound Bible with "Praise The Lord" tooled into the cover.

There were other numerous country and gospel music people there that day. I was astounded because I had a common stereotyped picture of professional recording artist—a portrait of miserable people wallowing in their success; drinking and doping to get up and get down and cope with the stage pressures; unhappy wretches in private life; finally alone and old with tarnished awards gathering cobwebs in stale rooms.

That image may fit some of the "successful" public idols, but that was not the case for these people at the prayer fellowship. These were genuine smiles and real tears as they testified of God's power. I was so astonished in fact that I said "Wow! Somebody ought to know about what's going on here."

Between the Lord, Marijohn, and myself, the idea soon surfaced and work began on a series of Christian experiences of famous Nashville personalities. The idea spread; the list grew quickly, not only including "pickers" and "wailers," but Nashvillians from various walks of life.

Obviously, the full chronicle of what Jesus Christ is doing in Music City would take many volumes, so this is just a select cross section of singers, songwriters, businessmen, musicians, producers, "idea people," and executives—the people who not only continue to make Nashville a music mecca, but people who are now even more interested in spreading a different light on the subject of music. There is even a story about a notorious prisoner now spreading this light behind prison walls.

Best wishes as you read and experience these accounts of some very special people who have finally discovered a very special Person.

I may never pass this way again, dear Lord;
Help me not to walk this way in vain,
But may each step, each word, each deed
Point others to You, I plead.
Help me, Lord, not to pass this way in vain.
                                              —Darryl E. Hicks

JOHN BROWN—
MAYBE STRINGBEAN DIDN'T DIE IN VAIN

Convicted in notorious murder case

Saturday night, November 10, 1973.

The Grand Ole Opry audience responded as Stringbean sang. Flashbulbs popped. Hands clapped. The old Ryman Auditorium shook with laughter as the overalled man went into his famous Stringbean shuffle.

This star of Opry and "Hee Haw" fame finished his set on the ten o'clock segment, singing "I'm Going To The Grand Ole Opry And Make Myself A Name." It was to be the last time he would sing on the stage.

He left the curtained spotlight as he entered, slow and certain—drinking in the applause—his gentle eyes flashing above that disarming smile. There was only one Stringbean.

11

Ever. The fans loved him. His gentle life touched fans of all ages with a bit of hillbilly magic.

People seemed to love everything he did. His scarecrow character on "Hee Haw." The "close to my heart...heart...heart" letter routine. Folks responded to his claw hammer banjo picking. He always brought down the house with a special down-home comedy.

He left the stage, and out in the parking lot, Stringbean slipped into the passenger seat of his Cadillac. His wife of twenty-eight years turned the switch to start the engine. Estelle chauffered him to each performance and television taping. He always left the driving to her.

Long as my wife gets me there, I don't tell her how to drive. She don't tell me how to fish. I don't tell her how to drive.

Her driving provided a backdrop for many impromptu jokes.

I can always tell when we's gettin' to town. We start runnin' into more people.

The two drove away from the auditorium toward their humble three-room red house on a 143-acre farm near Nashville.

The next morning, Grandpa Jones (also from Opry and "Hee Haw" fame) arrived at David and Estelle Akeman's farm to take his fishing and hunting buddy on a trip to Staunton, Virginia. There, he discovered the two bodies brutally murdered.

Nashville Metro Police cars screamed to the acreage. The pastoral setting became a montage of coroners and ambulances and flashing lights and newsmen.

Headlines blazed—**OPRY STAR STRINGBEAN AND WIFE MURDERED IN NASHVILLE.**

The next days shrouded Nashville with grief as country music people wept for one of their favorites. Letters and telegrams poured into the Opry office. There were sympathy cards—mountains of paper filled with expressions of love and sorrow.

David and Estelle's joint memorial service and burial

reflected their side-by-side life. It was simple. It was touching. Flower arrangements in the shape of a fish and a steering wheel were placed beside the two caskets. Many of Nashville's elite attended, weeping openly.

When the final tributes were read, the procession moved out into the street. Roy Acuff, String's close friend, described the somber scene.

It was a beautiful sight. One of the prettiest sights I've ever seen, in spite of the sadness. There they were—two hearses side by side, just as the two wonderful people lived. If our country can be touched by their tragic deaths, then maybe, just maybe, they didn't die in vain.

Even before the caskets were put in final resting places, the public outcry had spread. Authorities stepped up activities and investigations. Several suspects were questioned. The net began to tighten as several prime figures were under twenty-four hour surveillance.

12:55 P.M. January 16, 1974. The tense statement was aired that four men had been arrested. Handcuffed and under tight security, the Brown cousins—John, Doug, Roy, and Charley—were arraigned.

Previously fearing a Charles Manson-type execution ring, Nashville citizens breathed a sigh of tense relief to hear that it had been just an isolated robbery attempt by novices. Widespread fear was replaced with a hatred against the alleged murderers. Sacks of threatening letters reportedly flooded the Nashville postal system.

The trial for the Browns began October 28, 1974. On November 2, 1974, (just eight days before the first anniversary of the Akeman murders) at 9:20 P.M.—Saturday night—the jury brought the verdict.

Two cousins were convicted on two counts of first-degree murder. They were each sentenced to two consecutive ninety-nine year-terms in the Tennessee State Prison. It would be a minimum of thirty calendar years before either would be eligible for a parole hearing.

John Brown was one of those convicted of the brutal murders of two beloved people. He was no time-hardened killer, so the guilt of being part of such a hideous crime made the increasing burden of past mistakes an unbearable load. Hedged in by locks and walls and eternity—with no place to run and no where else to go with the heavy load, one day in 1977, the prisoner dropped on his knees.

Because of the current pending appeal, a weariness of being accused of getting a "jailhouse religion" just to get sympathy, and because of the hatred of so many people against him—for these understandable reasons, John Brown has never sought to publicize his shocking and tragic life-story, nor his salvation.

This, then is John Brown's narrative—for the first time ever in print.

John was born in Nashville, raised in Green Brier, a backwoodsy town about thirty miles north of Nashville. He was the oldest in the family of three boys and one little girl. His father worked as a masonry contractor. The rigors of hard labor left little time for affection.

Our family just never expressed any love outwardly. I guess there just wasn't a lot of love there.

Being the oldest, anything I attempted to do was never good enough. Dad often told me that I wasn't worth the salt in a slice of bread.

Before long, I saw that by showing rebellion I could get attention, so I did anything to upset my parents. Even as a little kid, I figured that getting the razor strap was better than getting no attention at all. I couldn't get them to love me, so I had to be satisfied with whippings.

Unbelievably, by the time John was eleven years old, the rebellion had spread to alcoholism. He had grown up fast and hard—by necessity.

When I was eleven years old, I got drunk at a sock-hop dance. I got in a fight. The police came. My dad came.

When he got me home, he took a 1 by 6 inch plank and

started beating me all over. I still wouldn't tell him where I got the liquor, so he finally carried me down to the jail.

From that time, I did anything I could to upset him. I felt that he had turned on me.

The obvious comparison that he saw from day to day intensified the rejection evident in his home.

As I was growing up, I would see the Shirley Temple movies. I would see the love in her home and I used to dream of having a family like that.

Even now, I watch the Waltons on TV and see the unity; it makes me wonder what it would have been like to be that way.

But it wasn't. When John was fifteen, 1965, his family moved to Michigan. There, as the drinking increased, education became more like a stone wall to him than a stepping-stone. When he reached sixteen, school was forgotten. Not only did he leave school, he left home. After the move to Pittsburgh to stay with a half-brother, the bottle became more of a problem. Drinking "buddies" that he coasted with not only had a matching thirst, but also had a penchant for permanently "borrowing" cars.

Landing in juvenile detention hall, John was finally given a chance to enter the armed forces, or spend time behind bars. Though his speedy enlistment and induction into the Marine Corps was less than voluntary, it temporarily gave him the discipline and rigid pattern that he needed so desperately.

During training he was married to his Pittsburgh girl friend. The newlyweds were stationed in California. As he was promoted up several ranks, John began considering a career in the Marines. It seemed at last he had found his niche.

Then the bottom fell out. On September 17, 1969, he was given a medical discharge for a previously undetected birth defect in his back. Though it was an honorable discharge, it was, to John, another in a lifelong list of rejections.

He went back to Michigan and began work as a chrome polisher in one of the big plants. Doing piece work, he eventually worked up to $500 a week. He and his wife soon celebrated the birth of a healthy son. Though his drinking had been kept somewhat in check, the everlasting "demon in the bottle" seemed to have a personal contract on John Brown. It began to create more and more problems.

Even at that time, I still didn't recognize that I had a drinking problem.

The social drinking and "good times" exploded when John was involved in a hit-and-run accident. After realizing what had happened, he panicked and left for Tennessee.

That really shook me. I laid off the bottle and got a job. My wife and son came to live with me after I got settled in Springfield, Tennessee.

Another son was born in March, 1971. At twenty, John was a hopeless alcoholic. Despite attempts to quit drinking, the old nemesis seemed inescapable.

I was down to making $2.70 an hour and using every penny to drink. There was no money left for groceries or rent. My wife was going hungry. We were getting ready to be kicked out of the place we were staying.

I drove her to stealing just to get food for the kids to eat. My drinking ruined life for her and my two sons. She finally left me in October, 1971. She didn't want a divorce—just wanted me to straighten up, but the divorce was inevitable. By this time, my habit had gotten so bad that I would go to sleep with a drink in my hand, and wake up with a drink in my hand.

Moving to Arlington, Virginia, he went through another job, business venture, and ill-fated illegal marriage. More rejection and alcohol. He returned to Nashville during June, 1973.

I came down here to go into the concrete business with my cousins; however, out of the first forty days I was here, I worked one day. All the rest I was out partying.

Until this time, I had been scared to mess around with drugs; now, though, I started fooling with grass and diet pills.

16

Even through this liquid-controlled time, he was searching. At times he attended churches seeking something better than what he was doing. One wonders what it would have been like today if he had surrendered at the altar instead of turning away from God's call.

I knew conviction. I knew that I needed to get saved, but I really thought that I enjoyed the drinking and all the partying, playin' pool, the bars, and dancing. Even the fighting—I thought that I enjoyed it all.

Though his criminal record was by no means filled with horrible crimes, it did contain a long list of disturbance and drunkenness charges. Getting drunk and "raisin' cain" became a way of life.

During the summer of 1973, John bumped into Debbie. The two had been grade-school sweethearts in Green Brier. They began dating in September, 1973. They attended church together at times, but neither made any decision.

November saw John hit an all-time binge. The effects were to be disastrous; the penalty costly.

I really got off into drinking. I couldn't hold a job. It was a continual "party." It was about this time—Saturday, November 10, that my cousin came over. He had an idea that would make us a lot of money.

I had drank all Friday night and got up drinking Saturday morning, trying to get rid of a hangover with whiskey and beer-chasers.

The more I drank that day, the better the possibility of making so much money sounded. They said that it would be easy. It sounded so simple.

We went to his brother's house to make plans—we would poke a gun in their face and they would hand over lots of money.

We continued to smoke grass, mixing it with pills and liquor.

That night we went to the Akeman's house. The next thing I knew, two innocent people were dead.

17

By the time I got home, I was stone-cold sober, scared to death realizing what had taken place. I felt horrible—didn't know what to do. Debbie had been the only one that I could talk to, but she couldn't help me figure out what to do.

I panicked. I left Tennessee and went to Detroit where I left some of my things with my parents. I had every intention of going to Canada and getting lost in the North Woods.

Then before I left, I started thinking about my two sons. If I was to get caught, I would never see them again, so I went to Pittsburgh to see them one last time.

By Thursday, though John was in Pittsburgh, the dragnet in Nashville was already in sight of the Brown boys. Debbie had been questioned. There was no evidence, but the death weapons were soon to be found.

That night, I called Debbie. She told me what was happening. She was scared for me and wanted me to come talk to the police. The next day I turned myself in after driving straight through. They questioned me most of the night then let me go for lack of evidence.

Knowing that the investigation was far from over, the cousins met and planned a strategy. The tight web of surveillance tightening, nerves reached the breaking point. Fearing that Debbie would talk, the cousins gave John an ultimatum—"Either you do something about her or we will!"

I married her out of desperation so she couldn't testify against me. She knew that we had been involved in the crime and that I would probably spend the rest of my life in prison, but she still loved me enough to go through with it. We were married on December 7, 1973.

I've always held it against myself that I married her under false pretenses, but as time has worn on, I've grown to love her. She's helped me more than anything.

The noose tightened. The pressure mounted. On December 14, John got drunk and totaled a car. He wasn't hurt, but was put in jail. Debbie worked to get him out. He promised to stop, but he continued drinking and taking pills. Finally giving up, Debbie attempted suicide on Christmas Eve; fortunately, John was sober enough to get her to a hospital in time. The situation seemed beyond hopeless.

The new year was anything but new or fresh. On January 16, a friend who was supposed to get rid of the guns, turned state's evidence. Immediately, the APB went out. As the tight-faced detectives snapped the metallic manacles on John's wrists, it symbolized the beginning of the end.

For the ten months until he was convicted, he occupied the "work house" under extremely tight security. Short "visits" from Debbie and his lawyer highlighted an unreal existence.

Debbie still vividly remembers the first time they talked after he was imprisoned.

We were allowed to visit in a place where we could talk to each other over a telephone and look at each other through a peephole.

I'll never forget that he looked me in the eye through the little window and said, "Debbie, whatever you do, I want you to promise me two things and keep them."

I said, "Okay, John, I'll do whatever you want."

"First, I want you to become a Christian, and second, I want you to watch after my two boys."

I told him that I would try.

John asked for magazines and books to read. Partly by accident, she fulfilled his request by impulsively purchasing an illustrated Bible. He was to read it from cover to cover.

Not too long after the initial visit, a minister, Sammy Phelps (then pastor of Nashville's Richland Nazarene Church), talked to Debbie. Not only was she living through the numb hell that the Browns had created, but continued to have her own problems with drugs.

That night, Brother Phelps talked to me about salvation. He made things so real, so important, so clear.

Feeling the soul-deep conviction welling up inside, she went home uncertain about what to do. Finally, with nothing else left to do, she knelt beside her bed and began to release all the problems of the past in a prayer.

I don't like living this way. I don't even know what I'm doing, but Jesus—if you'll forgive me of all the terrible things I've done, I promise You that I'll live for You all the rest of my life.

Instantly, the overwhelming peace of God flooded her life as she was forgiven. The Bible compares the salvation experience in many ways—"the new birth," "becoming a new creation," "passing from death unto life." Debbie didn't know all the theological phrases, but she knew that God had changed her. It was not only real, but was to last forever.

It was her new-found faith that carried her through the sanity hearing, through the sensationalized trial, through the threats against John's life, through the frustration of a marriage separated by walls.

It was Debbie's new-found faith that caused John to want what she had found. As he began reading the Bible that Debbie had brought, the case and trial became secondary to finding what was in the printed pages that had so changed his wife. He wanted to experience it too, but the clouds of guilt hovered over him.

I just didn't see how anyone like me could become one of His children. It was a bad hang-up, I know, but with the things I had done, I didn't see how the Lord could ever accept me as His son.

This apparent impossibility of ever finding a peace joined hands with the legal preceedings to form a seemingly inescapable prison—physically, mentally, spiritually.

The cousins planned to lay all the blame on John, since he had once been treated in a Michigan mental hospital for alcoholism. He planned to take all the rap, plead insane, spend a few years in an institution, then all would be free and forgotten.

I was trying to pull the wool over their eyes—to show symptoms of a psychotic. It was a good plan, but it didn't work out. I'm glad now that it didn't.

He lost the sanity—was ordered to stand trial as charged. Suddenly the plan was amiss; the camaraderie between John and his cousins vanished.

When I was pronounced sane, everybody panicked. I still trusted 'em, but they tried to lay everything on me. When the trial began on October 28, I didn't say much, not even to my lawyer. I figured that we still had it under control.

"We" obviously didn't include John. He had already "admitted" to the crime during the pre-trial sanity hearings. That backfired.

The three-ring circus in the courtroom was televised live outside of the courtroom and was crowded with media-coverage. When the jury brought the verdict and the courtroom cleared, John knew that the "whole monkey was on my back." By then, it was too late to tell what really had happened.

Under tight security (the threats had continued), John and Doug Brown were moved out to the penitentiary to begin serving the two consecutive ninety-nine year sentences. They were placed in separate "holes" (solitary confinement), in the "A" block (maximum security), where John eventually stayed for nineteen and a half months. This time, there was no escaping. There would be no running away from his problems, the past, or God.

Books seemed to be the only available outlet from the intense heat and boredom of the cell. He began studying. Dr. Shade at Immanuel Bible College offered the inmates at Davidson County Workhouse an opportunity to take Bible courses. John was the first in the workhouse to get the certificate. It was still an admitted "I want to show something for what I've done"—attitude, but it was a beginning. He developed a voracious appetite for learning; the years of rebellion had created an empty vacuum.

When he finally got out into "population" (out of isolation and maximum security) on June 16, 1976, he still was faced with the threats against his life. Many had said that he would be killed when he came in contact with the other inmates.

He went to work in the metal plant and at night attended night school. He took the GED tests and received his high school diploma—a notable achievement for one who had created havoc years before as a rebel-student. Undaunted and unharmed, he began working toward completion of his Associate of Arts degree from the University of Tennessee, Nashville (professors hold classes at the prison). He became an honor inmate, had a steady job, caused no problems, but God still hadn't won. Reformation and regeneration are similar but eternally different. Titus 3:5 says: "Not by works of righteousness which we have done, but according to his mercy he saved us, by the washing of regeneration, and renewing of the Holy Ghost."

The first committment to the Lord was on February 18, 1974, but he backslid. The final surrender and commitment came in early 1977.

There were quite a few problems. My wife was working at a hospital, but with all the extra bills, she didn't have money at all. Her car was old and undependable. So many things happened then at once that I just didn't have anywhere to turn.

The frustrations were magnified by not being able to do anything about them. His wife had been a living testimony that God was the only answer. Debbie's faithfulness through the trials were an ever-present monument to what God could do.

God had been convicting me since even before I got messed up in all of this. I still didn't know if God would even have me. I was afraid of rejection. I was afraid of being accused of getting a "jailhouse religion" like some of the guys do just to get out. But, finally, I threw up my hands and said, "Lord, I can't do anything about everything else, but I just want to turn my life over to You."

It wasn't overly-emotional or pseudo-dramatic, just a prayer of a man driven to his knees by a load of guilt and grief. Somehow, Jesus Christ the Healer got rid of all the old hurt. Jesus Christ the Redeemer replaced the ill-fated past with a clean future. Though men may never forgive, God loved the unlovable.

I still don't understand it. How in the world can God love me. I've just had to accept it. I'm not worthy of His love but He made me worthy. It would be hard for people to love me, much less God. I guess that's why I waited so long to give my heart to Jesus—I couldn't believe that He would accept and love me.

But He did, and He does. Psalm 51:1-14 is for me:

"Have mercy upon me, O God, according to thy lovingkindness: according unto the multitude of thy tender mercies blot out my transgressions.

Wash me throughly from mine iniquity, and cleanse me from my sin.

For I acknowledge my transgressions: and my sin is ever before me.

Against thee, thee only, have I sinned, and done this evil in thy sight: that thou mightest be justified when thou speakest, and be clean when thou judgest.

Behold, I was shapen in iniquity, and in sin did my mother conceive me.

Behold, thou desirest truth in the inward parts: and in the hidden part thou shalt make me to know wisdom.

Purge me with hyssop, and I shall be clean: wash me, and I shall be whiter than snow.

Make me to hear joy and gladness; that the bones which thou hast broken may rejoice.

Hide thy face from my sins, and blot out all mine in-
iquities.

Create in me a clean heart, O God; and renew a right
spirit within me.

Cast me not away from thy presence; and take not
thy holy spirit from me.

Restore unto me the joy of thy salvation; and
uphold me with thy free spirit.

Then will I teach transgressors thy ways; and sinners shall be converted unto thee.

Deliver me from bloodguiltiness, O God, thou God
of my salvation; and my tongue shall sing aloud of
thy righteousness."

Not only was John made acceptable in God's sight, and not
only was he adopted into God's family, but he began to see
material miracles happening. VA benefits helped ease Debbie's tense financial condition. John was baptized and joined
the Richland Nazarene Church. Even the prior hatred of
many of Stringbean's friends has been changed. Teddy
Wilburn is but one example; Teddy works with the "Seven
Steps" prison program.

*I was both skeptical and afraid the first night Teddy came
down. I wanted to say something, but I was scared to death
of him.*

Instead of hatred, Teddy showed a personal interest and
Christian concern for the man convicted of murdering a
beloved fellow-Opry performer. His personal love for the inmates has become a help and inspiration to the men behind
bars like John Brown.

Debbie and John have grown together during the "Seven

Steps" meetings and visits. Though it certainly isn't an ideal situation, God continues to give the strength to accept the circumstances. It was an especially touching scene when they were allowed to renew their marriage vows and dedicated themselves anew in the sight of God in the prison chapel on the third anniversary of a seemingly ill-fated wedding. Out of that dedication has come added reassurance that the Lord has everything in control. The past, present, and future are no problems for the surrendered Christian.

Yesterday is gone, though metallic reminders surround John Brown. Some people will never forget the horrible crime, but God has completely forgiven everything.

Today, John realized the unfathomable mercy of God. A person is more aware of God's love when he has lived with hate.

I praise God for putting me behind prison walls. I never would have given my life to Christ if He hadn't made me stop and look at where and who and what I was.

Tomorrow is uncertain. Appeal briefs have been filed but sometimes the legal formalities take years. Someday, perhaps, the real story will be told. Regardless, John is already a free man—prison walls or not.

I don't know what God has in mind for me. I will serve Him no matter whether I'm behind bars or not. I'm hoping to get a degree and become a Christian counselor. I want to try to prevent more kids from coming here. I want to turn them around before it's too late for them, too. I want to tell them that the only way to find peace of mind is not by doing what you want, but by accepting the Lord as Saviour.

Whatever happened, is happening, or will happen—God has proven that His grace is sufficient. That one fact makes this whole unbelievable story believable.

"But thanks be to God, which giveth us the victory through our Lord Jesus Christ" (1 Cor. 15:57).

CARL BUNCH—THE LAST TOUR
Drummer for Buddy Holly, Roy Orbison, Hank Williams, Jr.

Photo: Eddie Holder

Carl Bunch being interviewed by PTL Club co-host Henry Harrison.

It was 1975. Glimpses of the past flashed back in Carl Bunch's turmoil-filled mind. He was now just another faceless hitchhiker spending New Year's Eve in the Pascagoula, Mississippi Salvation Army. As he sat in the required church service (if he wanted a meal and bed), he kept thinking about bittersweet memories of his career as a rock and roll drummer who had touched the highest echelons of public acclaim; a career that once had brought him in contact with greats like Buddy Holly, Roy Orbison, Frankie Avalon, Hank Williams, Jr., Little Richard, Waylon Jennings—but now the cheering fans and brilliant moments were ragged remnants of a long-forgotten decade before.

As the clock neared midnight, the preacher, an old hills-of-

Virginia evangelist, handed out pieces of paper and asked the men to write down the things they wanted most in life. Carl wrote without hesitation—"I want my wife and babies back, and I want to sing again . . . for You, Lord."

The men were then instructed to place the papers in an old iron kettle (like the Salvation Army uses to collect for the needy), then they were to take another paper and write what they would give God in a trade for the things on the first paper. This time Carl began weeping.

It made me angry at first. I didn't have anything to trade. Finally out of desperation I wrote "me"—I realized it was all I had left.

That "me"—Carl Bunch—was born into quite different circumstances over thirty years before. He was James and Doris Bunch's premature baby—less than three pounds. He was loved and showered with "first baby" attention. By the time he was nine, his family had moved from Big Spring, Texas, to nearby Odessa. Also, by that time he knew that he wanted to spend his life in show business. He got the first tastes of stage-triumph as he and his sister, Cathy, became a top dancing team appearing all over Texas (slightly to the chagrin of Carl's father, a big, athletic building contractor).

After a football accident at thirteen, Carl was hospitalized with a bone tumor on his leg. That tumor developed and he was hospitalized for a year and a half. Determined to "lick" the wheelchair when he was finally released from the hospital, Carl decided to take up the drums to develop coordination in his legs and arms—at this time he was still intent on a dancing career.

I was never supposed to walk again, but the doctors decided to try an experimental operation—chipping pieces of my hip bone to replace the cancerous leg bone.

The operation was greatly successful. Soon the competition-oriented teenager found that his dancing dreams were to be completely overshadowed by his drumming abilities. He won a local talent contest and was asked to play drums for area well-knowns, Ronnie Smith and the Poor Boys, recorded on Brunswick Records, a subsidiary of Decca. This marked the beginning of an exciting and hectic period. West Texas was then becoming the hotbed for the rock and roll upsurge. Another Odessa group, Roy Orbison and the Teen Kings ("Pretty Woman," "Candy Man," "Only the Lonely") used Carl as a fill-in drummer from time to time. He began playing on television, recording sessions, dances, concerts—whatever came up. Carl also met such rising performers as Elvis Presley.

Carl was the drummer for the Poor Boys until the fall of 1958. Also in the group was Tommy Allsup (guitar). Future country great, Waylon Jennings, lived in a nearby West Texas town. Together the three became overnight superstars.

Tommy called me—said Buddy Holly (another West Texas native who was already "striking gold" with "Maybe Baby," "That'll Be The Day," and "Peggy Sue") had fired Jerry Allison and Joe B. Mauldin, the original Crickets, and he wanted us to join him in New York.

Without hesitation, Tommy, Waylon, and Carl joined the bespectacled rocker for the soon-upcoming 1959 Winter Dance Party national tour.

We all traveled together in the bus—Buddy and us (the "new" Crickets) along with Dion and the Belmonts, Frankie Sardo, Richie Vallens, and the Big Bopper. I was 17, suddenly traveling with the big rock and roll stars. It was like suddenly waking up in a different world. In just days I had what I wanted—to be a star. I knew what it was like to play in front of 8,000 screaming people—to get your clothes torn by the fans—the whole bit.

And we had fun—we were really just a bunch of kids—really pretty clean compared to the image people have of rock musicians. We always had funny nicknames for each other, called Dions group "Moron and the Bellhops," and them calling us "Bloody Holly and the Rickets." Buddy had names for

*everybody—he called me "Goose." One of the funniest things
was one night when Dion (from Brooklyn) tried to sing country music—"I nearly died when I tot youze had left me!"*

Then the tragedy struck. More than ten years later Don
McLean would immortalize it was "the day the music died"
in "American Pie." That day, or the early morning of
February 29, 1959, in Clearlake, Iowa, shrouded the nation.
Morning headlines shocked the world with the news that
Buddy Holly, Richie Vallens, and J. P. Richardson (the Big
Bopper) had been killed in a plane crash.

The three had flown ahead after the bus had broken down.
The remainder of the group, and the other singers, had stayed
behind until the bus could be towed in from the snowy
highway and fixed. Carl Bunch had to be admitted into a
nearby hospital that night with frozen feet from the time
spent in the disabled bus.

The headlines and funeral came and went, but the Crickets
were still under contract to complete the tour. Carl left the
hospital to rejoin the group. Ronnie Smith came from Odessa
to sing Buddy's part. However, overnight the frivolities turned to tears.

*After the tour started again, we played in Sioux City, Iowa.
My feet still weren't working well yet so one of Dion's band
members filled in for me. It was horrible—everyone broke
down in the middle of Buddy's songs. Even Waylon was torn
to pieces.*

The tour broke up in Chicago. Norman Petty, Jerry Allison,
and Joe B. Mauldin filed a suit against the group to get the
Cricket name back. Maria Elena (Buddy's widow), Tommy
Allsup, Waylon, and Ronnie Smith (Carl wasn't at the
meeting) decided to trade up the name for a Brunswick
Records contract. The group, The Jitters, recorded three
songs, had no promotion, and subsequently had three consecutive bombs.

*By June of 1959, we realized that we'd been had. Waylon
started his own group. I went into the army. Ronnie went to*

29

pieces—in two years he went from the top to glue-sniffing and finally hung himself with his T-shirt in a Rusk, Texas, mental institution.

Carl's two-year tenure with the army had a high point in 1961 when he won the All-Army Talent Show (an instrumental with Carl playing piano, drums, guitar, and bongos). Then after his honorable discharge that same year, he began a less-than-rewarding career playing one-nighters through the South and Midwest for small-time groups.

Finally, in 1967, Waylon heard I was playing in Omaha, Nebraska. He called and said Hank Williams, Jr. needed a drummer. I joined Hank—January, 1967, in Nashville.

The time spent in Nashville proved to be an oasis in an otherwise restless desert. During the year and a half with the Cheatin' Hearts, one of country music's tightest bands, Carl once again sustained a part of the fame that had long eluded him. He had songs published, met numerous friends who would be instrumental later (including Terry White who was then playing bass for "Whispering" Bill Anderson and had formerly been with Hank Williams, Sr., Hank Thompson, Leon McAuliff, Webb Pierce), made a movie, *A Time to Sing* (MGM), and most importantly, met Midge, his lovely wife, (daughter of Rosalie Allen, the "Queen of Yodelers" for RCA). They were married on March 19, 1969, WGM's Ralph Emery cracked, "The last of the Cheatin' Hearts has bit the dust!"

A dispute with Hank's manager ended Carl's time with the band. Carl and Midge spent six months in New York with Terry White and the Nashvillians. Then Waylon, who was by then becoming well-known as a country superstar, offered Carl a job via the telephone—wanted him to meet the Waylons in Phoenix, but when Carl arrived, there had been a mix-up—someone else had already been hired.

Thus began the turbulent seventies for Carl and Midge Bunch. With no job, and already this far West, Carl and Midge moved to California. He sold his drums—gave up performing as a musician—with hopes of becoming a serious writer and actor. He studied at the Theatre of the Arts (ex-M.A.S.H. headliner Larry Linville was one teacher). There was little success, however, and to sustain him until that "big break" came, Carl drove for the Playboy Limousine Service, for such notables as Goldie Hawn, Steppenwolf, Little Richard, Bill Bixby, Bill Cosby, Henry Kissinger, Carroll O'Connor, Sonny and Cher. Though he was known and near the stars, his lot had considerably fallen since the Buddy Holly days. He began sampling the star-offered drugs. Before long, the taste had developed into a heavy habit. The final crushing blow, quite literally, came in 1971, when after delivering Ann-Margaret, he came back to the garage. An accident due to a broken garage door spring left Carl with a smashed back. For two years he could not work. He and Midge had one child by then. Both parents were dropping deeper into drug habits.

By 1973, an amazing set of "coincidences" started—first a "science fiction," or so he thought, book, *The Late Great Planet Earth* caused him to begin reading the Bible. Then he heard a song, "Magnificent Sanctuary Band," of all places on the "Sonny and Cher Show." Then one Sunday morning he happened to watch evangelical TV-preacher, Jerry Falwell.

He was standing there with his hand in my face saying, "I don't care who you are, you could be a deacon in my own church, but if you don't know Jesus Christ, you are lost!"

The Lord spoke to me and said—"That's you!" I found myself on my knees screaming "Don't let me die! Don't let me die! Save me!"

That was the beginning of the two worst years in his life. His heart wanted to accept the Bible and God at face value, but the craving for drugs persisted. Midge gave birth to their second child. Finances continued to deteriorate. They were on welfare, but increasing amounts of dope came before food. Finally, the sheriff evicted them from their repossessed house.

We lived in our Oldsmobile station wagon—me, Midge, our

two kids, two dogs, and three cats—waiting for one more welfare check so we could go back to Alabama, where Midge's mother lived.

When we got the money we took off in the wagon. In the middle of the Arizona desert the car's wiring caught fire—burnt totally crisp—it even blew a big hole in the battery.

This was the beginning of the eeriest experience in Carl's memory.

We were stranded there—I was crying for the Lord to help us. The fire was out by then and I was trying to scrape off the burnt wires. Two men—I remember their first names only—Gordon and Richard—drove up—"Can we help you?" I said, "Can you rewire an automobile?" It was incredible—they said "Yes, we can." They had all the tools and rolls of computer wire—they worked all that morning and finished by 2 PM. We patched together the battery, started it, and they followed us to Odessa. I didn't know anything about angels then, but I truly believe in them now.

The Bunch bunch managed to raise more money in Odessa and continued to Alabama until another fire in Canton, Texas, left them stranded once again. A kindly Methodist minister bought tickets for Midge and the kids to go on to Alabama.

I planned to follow as soon as I could get the car fixed (this time it was the fuel pump that had started the fire). In my heart I knew that Midge and the kids would be better off without me. I had become a total bum—even using the children to get sympathy. I never believed a man could get so low.

Carl left the car and began hitchhiking towards Alabama, staying when he could in rescue missions. All he had left was his guitar and the memories of the last time he played the South with Hank Williams, Jr. He had been reduced from signing thousands of autographs to scrawling on nightly tattered house registers.

Then came the night at Pascagoula, Mississippi. New Year's Eve—1975. All he had left was a piece of paper with an inked "me."

When a person finally reaches the bottom, he must look up. Essentially, this happened to Carl. The New Year's promise to God grew from a midnight dream to a daylight reality. Within three days he had a job with the Mississippi Housing Authority (cleaning and painting). In three weeks Midge and the two children had rejoined him with a tearful renunion. Three months later he had been promoted to Young People's Sargeant-Major in the Salvation Army. He had not only gotten his voice back, but was singing a "new song" over Alabama, Louisiana, and Mississippi. And, within two years, he was chaplain in Monroe, Louisiana. For Carl and Midge, the singing and traveling was the beginning of today's "Dove's Nest Ministries."

Then some unusual circles completed. Carl's mother-in-law, who had recently become a "born-again" Christian, saw Terry White, from the Nashville and New York days, singing on the "PTL Club" television program.

She called me about Terry. I said, "You're kidding, there's no way!"

But I got curious enough to write to Terry in care of PTL. Within several weeks he called me—it was the most beautiful reunion. He had gotten saved before I did and began praying for me. He asked what I was doing and invited me to Charlotte. While there he inquired about a job for me. I was content where we were in Louisiana, but then I made the mistake of helping on the counselling telephones there at PTL. The first three people that I talked to—an 83-year-old lady, a 22-year-old girl, and another person—all were calls for salvation. I suddenly became a believer in Christian television and wanted to become a part of helping in such a fertile field.

Within weeks the move was made. He serves as a security guard and program aide at PTL. Midge works with the booking aspects of "Dove's Nest Ministries." He has appeared on the show to give his testimony (and saw a recent standing ovation to a medley of "born again" Buddy Holly tunes). Carl and Terry White have shared more reunions with other Nashville friends who have become Christians. One of Carl's favorites has been Little Richard—"If the Lord can save Little Richard and me—He can save anybody!"

Together, Carl, Midge, and their children, Corrina and James, are facing a beautiful future no one would have thought possible just a few years ago, especially Carl. They have placed their past, present, and future without reservation in quite capable hands.

Some people label the change in different terms—a transformation, "born again," "saved." There's two words that best apply to Carl and Midge Bunch—*new* and *miraculous*!

"When someone becomes a Christian he becomes a brand-new person inside. He is not the same any more. A new life has begun!

All these new things are from God who brought us back to himself through what Christ Jesus did. And God has given us the privilege of urging everyone to come into his favor and be reconciled to him.

For God was in Christ, restoring the world to himself, no longer counting men's sins against them but blotting them out. This is the wonderful message he has given us to tell others.

We are Christ's ambassadors. God is using us to speak to you: we beg you, as though Christ himself were here pleading with you, receive the love he offers you—be reconciled to God.

For God took the sinless Christ and poured into him our sins. Then in exchange, he poured God's goodness into us!" (2 Cor. 5:17-21, LB).

DON BUTLER—THE DIRECTOR
Former recording great,
now Gospel Music Association's top executive

Photo: Gospel Music Association

Sitting on the black upholstered chair in his office, Don Butler looks the part that he plays. He is immaculately dressed in a vested suit. His white hair adds a touch of dignity, and his friendly eyes dance when he speaks about three favorite subjects: the Lord, his family, and Gospel music. The above mentioned "part" affects almost everyone in the industry, for he is the Executive Director of the Gospel Music Association and the Gospel Music Hall of Fame.

Though it's a long way from the home where he picked up the rich Southern drawl to the office in Nashville, it's perfect and fortunate that the Director casts him for this part.

The curtain opened for Don Butler in Atlanta, Georgia.

After public education in that city, he attended Emery University and the University of Georgia where he majored in Business Administration and/Retail Merchandising.

He took an active role in the church and studied voice all through junior high and high school. He sang with some of the top glee club groups in the nation as a featured soloist. Hopes remained high for becoming an operatic singer, but something dramatic changed these hopes quickly.

I used to go in the building in Atlanta where they did live radio shows. I'd look through the glass at whoever was performing. One day the broadcast featured the Rangers Quartet.

Wow! I found the music fascinating. It had a beat, not as much as now, but it was different from church music and different from the opera that I was used to. I became quite stricken with it. Denver Crumpler began telling me all about the Gospel quartet business. He told me of the Vaughn and Stamps Singing Schools. I finally went to one of the "singing normals." As a result, the "bug" bit me!

I had studied voice for fourteen years, but from that time on I didn't care about anything else but Gospel music.

So, a lifetime love affair began, though it was to continue only on a part-time basis for several years. After graduating, Don went with R. H. Macy, the large chain department store. He was assigned to the Atlanta store in merchandise marketing, in charge of buying for the main store at first—later for the branch stores also.

After an up-the-ladder venture into this marketing business, Don decided that life held more for him than the succession of salesmen and buying trips and late-night headaches.

I just finally got tired of the merchandise rat race: the low pay, long hours, the "ulcer factory." I wasn't feeling the satisfaction one desires out of life.

After earlier part-time ventures in broadcasting, Mr. Butler went back into radio in 1955—this time as a livelihood, first on WEAS, then on WGUN (both fifty-thousand watt stations). He started with a daily five-and-a-half hour black Gospel program. He also did a kiddie show, "Uncle Don's Birthday Party!" Later, white Gospel was added to his crowded air-time schedule.

Progressing up the broadcast industry ladder, Don went into sales and managing, at the same time doing television commercials and variety programs. He remained active in church work, having always felt the urge to be in some form of the ministry. He became ordained and served as an assistant pastor, minister of music, and finally as pastor—simultaneously supporting his family with the radio-TV jobs. Church work, though tedious, was a financial labor of love.

After several years, Mr. Butler had advanced to being national sales manager for five stations, manager of an Atlanta station, and assistant to the president of a radio corporation, the Rivers Stations Network (Florida and Georgia).

Again, as the work began to press in, a change was needed. This time, however, full-time Gospel music won against all competitors. Again, as twice before, Don Butler experienced a meteoric success.

We had formed the Sons of Song in 1957, but disbanded in 1958 after an automobile accident. We reorganized in 1961 as a trio—Bob Robinson (formerly with the LeFevres), Calvin Newton (Oak Ridge Boys), and myself (Revelaires). It was a very unique group. We tried to be innovators—style-setters with clothing, arrangements, recordings.

Up to that time, the Gospel music business had been "marking time" for several years. The Sons of Song broke in with perfect timing, creating a sound so different that throngs of people noticed. Though the group stayed together only from 1961 to 1963, during that short span they appeared on the first television shows from Hollywood; they were also the first to record in Hollywood on the Sacred label. They were featured in Phil Kerr's musicals in the Pasadena Music

Hall. The sky-rocketing trio became the first white Gospel group to tour with Mahalia Jackson on a regular basis. They toured with other legendary names, including Sonny James. Obviously, daring to be different paid off above all expectations.

After more than two years of non-stop running, the group broke up. Don went to work shortly after as business administrator for the Blackwood-Stamps Enterprises (Skylight-Sing Records, Stamps Publishing and Gospel Quartet Publishing), representing J.D. Sumner and James Blackwood until 1965.

Returning to Atlanta, Don managed the Statesmen Quartet's Enterprises and music publishing company. In Atlanta, again he took part-time pastorates.

1972 marked the year of the move to Nashville when Mr. Butler joined the Sumar Talent Agency where he used his talents until October, 1976.

Though Don Butler doesn't mention the dramatic events, even he must often look back in amazement at the astounding array of jobs in his past—each one a perfect and separate foundation-layer for the building God was preparing this man to be.

In October, 1976, Don, who had been chairman of the board of trustees of the Gospel Music Association, was put on a salary as the full-time Executive Director of the GMA and the Hall of Fame.

Looking back now from the place God has entrusted to him, Don Butler reflects on several life-changing experiences:

I became a Christian when I was a child, but until 1965 I just played Christian. I finally looked at myself, saw myself wasting both time and talent.

For many Christians, things often tend to get all walled up—we ask: "Why are there no results? Why nothing lasting or satisfying?" I kept looking at everybody else rather than myself. At last, I quit playing Christian and church and got down to business. I realized that if I was ever going to get anyone to listen to me talk or sing about Jesus that I was first going to have to be sincere and honest with myself. I dedicated my life completely to the Lord then. It's been a lasting experience.

Another period of self-examination with even more beautiful results happened in January, 1974.

I had massive heart attacks in 1973—November, so in January of 1974, I had open-heart transplant-surgery with three artery bypasses. They said that I died in surgery—the doctor and nurses raced down the hall with bed, bottles, and needles to the coronary intensive care unit to try to save me.

I knew that I was dying—it became one of the most beautiful experiences a man could ever imagine. All my life I had wondered "Would I go in a hurry? Would I see angels?" I think these are normal questions for any Christian.

When I knew that I was dying, the only thing that happened was feeling the greatest sense of peace I have ever experienced.

There are two Scripture verses that speak of this peace: Romans 5:1 says, "Therefore being justified by faith, we have PEACE with God through our Lord Jesus Christ." Philippians 4:7 talks about the same thing: "And the PEACE of God, which passeth all understanding, shall keep your hearts and minds through Christ Jesus."

This peace was only disrupted by one thought—I didn't want to come back. I had no remorse; no regrets. It was the most peaceful feeling—beyond description. The only thing I wanted to do before leaving was to tell my wife and children good-bye, but I didn't want to come back. I was going to heaven—I was so happy!

In the coronary unit, the personnel worked furiously, finally succeeding in bringing Don Butler back to life. An obvious question: what was it like to transcend two worlds and live to tell of it?

When I came back, and was able to talk, I told my wife that I was almost gone! I had almost left her, but God had spared my life for some reason, even if I didn't know why.

From that time on, I've had no fear of death or leaving. I have had a chance to really look at some things and get my priorities set—to try to see why the Lord let me live. I've tried to look at every day of my life and say—"Well, Lord, is this the day you saved me for?" It's brought such a richness to my life.

When they performed surgery again on my heart later, I wasn't afraid, because I figured that if it came out okay I'd get a new heart; if not, I'd get a new body!

Mr. Butler has since fully recovered, and the most obvious reason for his being alive today is his new ministry—the inner workings of the Gospel Music Association. He belies his former heart weaknesses by going fast-paced everyday, scurrying from meetings with music executives to nonstop telephone calls—mostly centered around the subject he loves—Gospel music.

Music is a common denominator. It breaks down barriers. By having this common denominator as a universal language, we can come into contact with almost everyone; we can tell others of the goodness and saving grace of God.

We have so many facets in Gospel music reaching out for people—black Gospel, blue-grass, white Southern quartet style, contemporary Jesus music, middle of the road/easy listening.

All of these areas are literally exploding with new ideas, new interests, new artists; therefore, it's only fitting that a man who has experienced all facets of the spectrum should now be the avid spokesman of the industry. He was very instrumental even in the inception in 1964 when the GMA was created to encourage, support, promote, propagate, and perpetuate the cause of Christ through Gospel music. He now is the focusing influence that vocalizes the credo.

We feel now that the primary purpose of the GMA is the promotional area, to help people better deliver Gospel music to the masses, and also to be a voice for all styles of Gospel music to be heard and represented.

Sorry to say, we have people in various endeavors of our industry who don't know what the others are doing; there seems to be so few lines of communication established. The GMA is trying to throw out these lines to all so we can get them all drawn in closer to each other.

We're all singing and saying the same message—Jesus Christ. We're all doing it for the same purpose—to win people and encourage Christians, so all of us need to pull together.

The GMA wants to be the umbrella of this total effort as we all get closer together in our sharing and witnessing.

According to Mr. Butler, the GMA is, in addition to this promotional thrust, trying to use the educational tools available through radio seminars on different areas of Gospel music.

We've established a speaker's bureau through which knowledgeable persons go to the mass medias, civic organizations, clubs, churches, and explain the Gospel music story. This tool exposes new people to our industry and widens the circle. We want more and more people to be touched by Gospel music.

One gigantic project looming in full view for this visionary man is the soon-to-be-built Gospel Music Association Hall of Fame.

At first, many people thought that the Hall of Fame was being set up to praise men, but I think now everyone is seeing that it's a testimony to what God has done and is doing through His music.

It's going to contain a library/information center for the whole world—laymen as well as professional people, students as well as ministers—to have at their fingertips information about the authors and stories of hymns and Gospel songs. The information center will contain the sounds, styles, and publications in other words, a history of Gospel music.

Also, in the building we will have a chapel open every day. There will be no charge for the library or chapel, but there will be an admission charge for the museum and display area to support the library, chapel, and offices of the GMA.

Don Butler speaks with an unusual authority—a charisma that builds. His message is one of love, and his eyes sparkle with excitement as he speaks about his ministry.

The GMA is becoming a meeting place for a great many Christians. We're experiencing an explosion not just here but in all of Gospel music. Right before Carter's inauguration, a reporter for the Los Angeles "Times" called me to comment about Gospel music—it was written up on the front page. That's just one instance of the many stories; it's the same in the Chicago "Tribune," CBS's "Who's Who," BILLBOARD, CASHBOX. Our whole industry has gone international.

It's great just being a part of it—seeing the GMA branch out and bring the music industry people closer together.

Don Butler remains living proof that Jesus is a saving, loving, caring director on this life-stage. God knew all along what the script was, even back when Don struggled against the dissatisfaction and fruitlessness, even then God knew that someday His servant would be fitly prepared for a giant task, executive director for an industry that every day takes Jesus Christ to a needy, troubled, searching world.

JESSI COLTER—A NEW DIRECTION
Wife of "Outlaw" Waylon Jennings,
award-winning singer and songwriter "I'm Not Lisa"

Photo: Utopia Productions Inc.

She's a pretty picture of contrasts. Onstage, she looks tiny and frail beside bearded band members and semi-truck loads of sound equipment, yet her voice booms past audience applause. Shimmering spotlights make her white dress stand worlds apart from the dimly-lit musicians. Truimphant, she gently retreats from the thundering crowd. Though the denimed backstage crowd fills the dressing rooms with noise and clattering cans, she emits a peacefulness unflurried by the smoke-filled corridors. Even her marriage to country-rock giant Waylon Jennings is a daring paradox, because though the media pushes his "Outlaw" image, her warmth and inner peace reaches past the million-dollar scenario. The whole picture of Jessi Colter, from religious childhood to atheistic youth to new-born Christian, is a composite study of contrasts.

Born in Mesa, Arizona, she was the sixth of seven children born to Helen and Arnold Johnson. Named Mirriam, she grew in an unusual family. Arnold Johnson (now seventy-nine, living in Nashville) built precision-engineered race cars for the Indy 500 races. He traveled for several years working and sometimes driving the powerful machines.

He went off the road for Mama and started an auto/body shop in Mesa. He also worked as a cotton harvester to make a living. Later, he was a mining engineer in some copper and molybdenum mines near Ray, Arizona.

My mother accepted the Lord when she was twenty-seven and went into evangelism. She also pastored for twenty-five years of her forty-four years in the ministry.

Jessi's church-centered childhood gave both the impetus and opportunity for the young, dark-eyed girl to begin her musical training.

I was eleven years old when I started playing the accordion and piano and also singing in church. I guess that it was for the lack of anyone else to do it, but it was also great discipline for me.

Helen Johnson became a great inspiration for her family, but she was also a rebel in the church movement. She was a Pentecostal who believed in tongues, the spiritual gifts, casting out demons. This evangelistic pioneering did not fit in well in a traditionally Mormon town.

We were made fun of and teased a lot, but I learned real early that I did not belong so I had to toughen up. I had to go inside and be creative. Spiritually, I was loyal to Mother and the church, but I had no personal experience.

At eighteen, she left home. The small-town girl met and married Duane Eddy who was then experiencing a sky-rocketing career from his "Rebel Rouser" guitar stylings. From Mesa, she went to New York City, then moved to

Beverly Hills, California. With Duane, she mixed with "names" like Dick Clark, Chubby Checker, and the like. It became a make-believe world of famous friends and tinseltown parties. She also began touring with Duane.

Quickly the changes came. The renowned husband and wife celebrated the birth of a daughter. Success continued to shine brightly, but new intellectual ideologies were touched and taken. Back at home, Helen prayed for the daughter who was trading her old beliefs for new ones.

I began searching, finally settling on an existentialist philosophy—"live for now." Everything was in abstractions. It made so much sense at the time. I had reasoned past the need for a God, and I felt sorry for my Mother and her outdated religious beliefs. I had outgrown the Lord and went as far away from Him as possible.

From that point, I spent two years as an atheist with no limits except to do whatever I wanted.

Helen's heart was broken in 1969 when her daughter divorced Duane. She still prayed for the once-small girl who used to play the piano for so many church services, this same young lady who now embraced the "man is his own end—there is no God" tenets.

After living in Los Angeles for a year after the divorce, Mirriam and her daughter, Jennifer, moved briefly back to Arizona. Soon she began dating country-star Waylon Jennings. She had met him while still with Duane Eddy. They had sung together some then, but it was after both went through their own separate divorces that they began dating.

I was fascinated by this mysterious man. The country music world had been pretty prejudiced against him, but he kept working and hitting and finally ended up on top.

She began traveling with Waylon. Mirriam became Jessi, "borrowing" her name from a distant relative—Jessie Colter—who had been an old west, James Gang outlaw. Jessi and Waylon were married and in October, 1971, moved to Nashville. Soon Jessi said good-bye to her own musical career to be housewife and mother, Jennifer and Waylon's children, Terry, Julie, and Buddy—all became a full-time occupation. She put her energy behind her husband and his spiraling career.

In successive years the "Outlaw" movement caught hold as Waylon, struck recording "gold" again and again on the country and pop charts, not only selling stacks of discs but also winning numerous industry awards. As Waylon teamed with Willie Nelson, the Texas sound swept the country music circuit.

Jessi, after homemaking for several years, once again began recording with a mound of stored-up energy. Within months of her mid-seventies debut, she poured out hit after hit—"Diamond In The Rough," "What's Happened To Blue Eyes," "Storms Never Last." Perhaps the best and biggest was "I'm Not Lisa," which rated the monumental number one slot on the *Record World* charts. The million selling "Outlaws" album featuring Jessi, Waylon, Willie, and Tompall Glaser was a phenomonal success.

The problems came when Jessi began seeing some loopholes in her atheistic philosophy during this time. One common misconception the public makes is that success and fame automatically brings happiness as the star basks in man-made sunshine; often, however, the exact opposite is true.

I was up against the wall so many times. One day, as I faced another big problem, I caught myself saying—"Well, I guess there's always God." I had gone so far in not believing in Him. The pendulum started swinging back.

I began trying to find the answers through metaphysics, but I soon got very impatient with the teacher—it was so slow; one fact at a time. I needed answers, so I knew this wasn't gettin' it.

I began opening the Bible and studying it myself. My experience and church background as a child made it easier to walk into a personal faith later on.

46

I started wanting to try what little I believed to see if it worked. My first test of faith came soon. I was a chain smoker. I had tried to stop many times before, but I didn't have the will power to quit. It was a simple thing, but I finally prayed about it—the smoking. When I did pray I felt like I was betraying my intellectual beliefs, but as a result of that first little bit of faith I was able to stop smoking. I felt surer then.

I began studying the Bible more for my own heart's comfort. This slowly built my faith and my trust in the Lord.

Jessi's relationship with her mother began to improve, a warm, storybook mother/daughter love. As everything seemed to be patched together, Helen Johnson died. For so long, even during the atheistic years, she had been a secure source of inspiration, a spiritual sort of leaning post when the world became unbearable. Faced with the absolute and tragic loss of her mother, Jessi had to go one way or go back to the unbelief. Small tests were behind her—the large ones beginning. She had to accept God's plan, or reject it.

I had swung so far from good to evil, so intensly, that I knew I had to reach a point when I had to go one way or the other; either that or go crazy. The pendulum was swinging, and I reached the point when I had to commit my will. I made a will-choice, Godward.

It hasn't been easy nor unstormy since that D-Day in Nashville, but Jessi has never been the same. Like a spreading warmth—her friends, associates, fans, and family swiftly noticed the change. Even her professional career found a dynamic new direction. She began writing a new brand of love songs. The "Mirriam" album (on Capitol Records), her first Christian disc, was a bountiful statement of her new faith—songs rich in sincerity: "Put Your Arms Around Me," "Let It Go," "New Wine."

The album is self-explanatory. It's my personal experience, love songs to the Lord. Perhaps if one didn't know about me, they might think I was talking to a man, I guess they could

be taken either way depending upon the person listening.
They seem to be received with peace, and we all need peace,
comfort, and love.

On the road or at home, she emits a gentle peace. About his
wife of seven years, Waylon recently said, "Jessi's the *best*
woman I've met. She's the *best person* I've ever met. She's
the *most talented person* I've ever met." Coming from
Waylon, who has mixed with the best and worst of each
category, *that's* some statement. It's also a fitting tribute to
one special woman's faith. Somehow, in the midst of the
whirlwind-turbulent pace, Jessi keeps everything
together—her family, her career, and her faith. It doesn't
always come easily.

There is good in every situation. I look for that.

The Apostle Paul said the same thing back in the First
Century: **I have learned to be satisfied with what I have. I
know what it is to be in need, and what it is to have more than
enough. I have learned this secret, so that anywhere, at any
time, I am content—whether I am full or hungry, whether I
have too much or too little. I have the strength to face all con-
ditions by the power that Christ gives me.**

—Philippians 4:11-13, Paraphrased

Jessi has lived so many lives: little Mirriam, daughter of
unique parents; that pretty Johnson girl who might easily
have ended up Mrs. Donald Schwartz living on Second and
Hobson in Mesa, Arizona; the flashy singing idol married to
music greats; intellectual atheist with increasing doubts.
Thank God, the story didn't end at any previous point. With
the newborn faith now so evident, the best is yet to come.

The stage is set for a career no longer limited by human
boundaries. Whatever God touches, He perfects; so for this
young Christian who has already sped down so many
avenues, walking on Perfection Street doesn't seem so hard
for this determined lady and her determining Lord.

For her, life has a new direction, a new determination, and a
new destination. For Jessi Colter, life will never be the same.

DALLAS FRAZIER—WELCOME HOME
Hall of Fame songwriter—
"Alley Oop," "There Goes My Everything"

If money, prestige, and fame could have bought happiness, Dallas Frazier would have been one of the most cheerful persons in the world. If ever there was an extraordinary songwriter, Dallas Frazier filled the mold. It was 1975. He was soon to be inducted into the Nashville Songwriters Hall of Fame with fellow greats: Mel Tillis, John D. Loudermilk, Carl Belew, Moon Mullican and Curly Putnam. He had been voted the songwriter of the Year in 1967. His songs were spectacular hits being recorded by giant singers—Elvis Presley, Connie Smith, Charley Pride, Jack Greene, Charley Rich, Jerry Lee Lewis, and Tanya Tucker.

But during 1975, the success became increasingly hollow. There were innumerable problems in Dallas' life. He was being tormented by torments only a chronic-alcoholic can know. For a songwriter with seemingly unlimited talent and success, the "good life" had become a vicious unfocused existence.

Though he tried and tried, Dallas just couldn't outrun the God who loved him and the prayers of a wife who wouldn't stop praying. That race, with its successes and its failures, provides one of the most exciting accounts of God's undying faithfulness.

Dallas was born in 1939 in Spiro, Oklahoma, a scene not unlike John Steinbeck's "Grapes of Wrath," especially with the Okie pilgrimages to California when Dallas was three years old where the Fraziers worked in cotton fields. The family eventually settled in the Bakersfield area where, although his parents separated, Dallas first met the musical influence of his uncle—Matin Laughlin.

Although in most areas he was just like any other patched-jeans schoolboy, from an early age he was very musically inclined. His parents didn't have any special talents in that direction, but were country people; therefore, the music of Hank Williams and Lefty Frizzell was the music Dallas knew as a child.

When he was barely ten years old, Dallas began writing songs. Two years later, realized an early dream by winning an area talent contest.

We lived on a ranch near Bakersfield. I heard about the contest, so I finally talked my Dad into taking me into town so I could sing. I remember I sang "Hillbilly Fever."

But winning the contest wasn't all that happened. Ferlin Husky was living in Bakersfield at the time. It was 1952 and he was just starting to have some hit songs—just signed with Capitol Records. Anyway, he heard me and asked me if I wanted to join his show as a featured act!

Though he was young, his parents realized that music was his dream so they didn't stand in the way of this sudden opportunity. He moved in with Ferlin, attending school between travels. Although he couldn't work the night clubs because of his age, the audiences at the big country dances loved the antics of the talented youngster—an unusual mixture of pre-teen and professional.

The public exposure and success led to a recording contract with Capitol when Dallas was fourteen. Just being on the label was a prestigious and coveted position for seasoned artists; a phonomenon for one so young. He wrote many of the songs that he recorded. "Love Life at Fourteen" and "Ain't Ya Had No Bringin' Up At All" experienced some success and radio airplay for the prodigious Capitol artist.

I always had a dream to be successful. I believed in myself even though there were many discouraging times later. I just fixed my mind on succeeding. As a kid, we were exceptionally poor, so I had a thing of wanting to obtain financial success as much as anything. I guess I was obsessed with succeeding.

Ferlin didn't drink at the time and made an attempt to keep his young protégé away from the wrong people, but the night-life made an early influence.

He treated me right, but any kid who goes into show business for a living and is around all the things in show biz has to grow up quickly.

When Ferlin moved to Nashville with his first national hit record, Dallas stayed in California to work with a local promoter, "Cousin" Herb Henson. At the same time a tremendous avenue opened; he started appearing as a regular act on "Cliffie Stone's Home Town Jamboree," one of the top two television programs in the entire Southern California area. It originated in Los Angeles. Dallas was a featured singer with regulars Johnny O'Brien, Tommy Sands, and Molly Bee.

This fantastic opportunity to work with Cliffie Stone, songwriter, promoter, and Ernie Ford's personal manager, lasted for four years, until the show went off the air when Dallas was eighteen years old. After the television program stopped, Dallas continued playing clubs in California and Phoenix.

Another important milestone that year—1958—happened when his girl friend, Sharon (also eighteen), became his lovely June bride. Little did they know what the future held for them despite the early successes.

Money was always a problem. It would seem that I could have had plenty, but because I wasn't twenty-one yet, I wasn't able to play a lot of the choice places. Because of the television show and recording contracts, I could have been booked into the top clubs, but as a minor I was limited in where I could go.

While still a teenager, Dallas wrote a comedy song, and he met a singer who instantly liked the song. The *song*—"Alley Oop;" the *singer*—Gary S. Paxton; the *result*—a million-selling smash national hit record.

I met Gary in 1960 at the American Recording Studio in Hollywood. He had just moved to Hollywood from Oregon, and I knew that he had had a lot of record success as one of the members in the group "Skip and Flip." He was doing novelty blues and the kind of music I was into—I guess we would call it "funky" today. Anyway, we sort of hit it off since we had the same musical likes and dislikes.

I wrote "Alley Oop" before I met Gary, and just shortly after I met him, I played the song for him; it knocked him out! He was really inspired to cut it right away. He got some musicians together; he did the voice—called the group the Hollywood Argyles.

Gary did all the organization getting the record out. Within weeks it was a million seller—real quick. I don't even know how many it sold, but it was the biggest thing to happen around Los Angeles for a long time. I do remember that at one time, three different versions of it (it was recorded by other artists including the Dynasores) were rated number 1, number 18, and number 50—all the same week in BILLBOARD.

By the time Dallas reached the legal age of twenty-one, he had already experienced a national reknown of which most people only fantasize. In his few years, he had realized dream after dream. But . . . *something* was missing.

I had a terrible need. I'd been drinking real heavy. I was living wrong and dangerously.

I guess the problems got the heaviest when a close friend of mine got into a pretty bad accident. It got to me. Some other things were happening and, looking back now, it was mainly that I was under conviction. I can attribute part of that to a Billy Graham Crusade that I saw on television at my sister's house; the seed was planted then.

Two or three weeks later, I had moved back to the Bakersfield area—McFarland. Pete Pyle, a close friend back in school, invited me to church, the Apostolic Pentecostal Church. during the service I broke down and accepted the Lord in a glorious way. God really saved me. It's a miraculous thing for any person to be saved from his sins, but it's really a miracle when it happens to you.

Well, I felt like I should get away, completely out of the show biz life I had been in, so I dropped it altogether and started working in a grocery store. I was sort of that small town's hero, so you can imagine the immediate response—"He's lost his mind!"

Sharon was caught by surprise at what happened to me, but it wasn't long afterwards that she accepted Him, too. Together we began our life in the Lord.

Unfortunately, salvation is just the start. From that point of contact, the actual battle begins. Dallas and Sharon knew that the "born again" change was real, and began serving their Saviour wholeheartedly. Dallas felt a yearning to be a preacher, an ambition that consumed him at the time. He studied the Bible; he even preached several times.

My zeal was in the right direction, but I was getting way ahead of the Lord.

During 1962, Sharon and Dallas moved to Portland, Oregon, where spiritual tragedy struck suddenly.

I don't know how it happened, but I guess that it was

through my weakness and lack of strength. Anyway, I backslid. I didn't fall away from my faith in God, but I did fall away from being loyal to the Lord.

I had previously had a terrible problem with alcohol before I was saved, so when we began to have financial problems in Oregon I got depressed. It was just a "skin of our teeth" existence. finally, I began drinking again.

Not long after that, Ferlin Husky came to Portland. It was late '63. I went out to the show just to say "Hi." He asked me if I would move back to Nashville, Tennessee, and write songs for him.

I was down and in bad shape—financially and spiritually--in everyway at the time, so it occurred to me that it was the thing I needed at the time. Actually, I accepted his offer gladly. It was an escape.

Ferlin gave Dallas and Sharon enough money to move and get started in Nashville. Though the problems were far from over, a spectacular songwriting career began to skyrocket.

I had been writing for years before, but for the first time, I really pursued songwriting as a job. I still believed in myself and knew that if I got in and really worked at it, the law of averages was on my side.

Previously I had never thought of writing as an out-and-out occupation, but when I came to Tennessee, I really got tuned into what was happening in the music market.

His "tuning in" education started as soon as he arrived in Music City, and within a year the industry started to see his efforts traveling from pencil to tapes to records to radio stations to stores—all over the nation. In 1964, "Timber I'm Falling" (co-written with Ferlin Husky) hit most of the country charts. During 1965, Charley Rich had a giant rock tune with "Mohair Sam." Additionally, many "name" artists started recording Frazier songs.

Jack Greene cut a number one gold country hit in 1966--"There Goes My Everything." Dallas won the Songwriter of the Year in 1967 for that song, which has since become a country and pop classic that almost everyone has sung, including the late Elvis Presley.

Obvious to all in the music industry, Dallas Frazier's flame of fame was flickering brightly.

I wrote in volume. I figured that a lot of songs had a better chance to be recorded than just a few. Even though I was starting to get quite a few songs cut, I was also drinking even more. It was really getting a hold on my life.

Through it all, Sharon stuck with me. She did an excellent job raising our three girls (Melody, Robin, and Alison) though I failed them. She had plenty of reasons to leave me, but she didn't—she stayed faithful to me and to the Lord.

The lusty taste for alcohol became more of a full-time threat, but somehow the zeal and energy for songwriting increased. That zeal was well founded; a long list cannot even hold all the hit songs written by Dallas—most of them top ten country or pop recordings:

1967—"Ain't Had No Lovin'" (Connie Smith)

1968—"If My Heart Had Windows" (George Jones)

1969—"Son of Hickory Holler's Tramp" (O. C. Smith) and (Johnny Darrell)

"Johnny One Time"—co-written with Doddle Owens (Brenda Lee)

1970—"All I Have to Offer You Is Me" (Charley Pride) a national number one hit co-written with Doddle Owens "I'm So Afraid of Losing You Again" (Charley Pride) another number one song written with Doddle Owens

1971—"I Can't Believe That You've Stopped Loving Me" (Charley Pride) a number one tune co-written with Doddle Owens "Where Is My Castle?" (Connie Smith)

1972—"Touching Home" (Jerry Lee Lewis) co-written with Doddle Owens

Where Did They Go, Lord?" (Elvis Presley) with Doddle Owens

1973—"If It Ain't Love (Let's Leave It Alone)" (Connie Smith) "Just For What I Am" (Charley Pride) a number one chart-buster written with Doddle Owens

"Until My Dreams Come True" (Jack Greene) another national number one song for Dallas

1974—"Dream Painter" (Connie Smith) co-written with Whitey Shafer

"The Baptism of Jesse Taylor" (Johnny Russell) and (Oak Ridge Boys) co-written with Whitey Shafer

"Ain't Love A Good Thing" (Connie Smith)

What's Your Mama's Name Child" (Tanya Tucker) a number one song across the nation co-written with Earl Montgomery

Through the years since, the listing of phenomenal successes is endless (country supersinger Connie Smith alone recorded over fifty of Dallas' songs). His own recording hit numerous charts across the nation—("Elvira" on the Capitol label was number one on pop stations in Houston and Atlanta; "Big Mable Murphy" on RCA was a smash in some areas of the country). But, as the fame mounted . . . so did the traumas.

My mind started giving me a bad time. I went so far down that at one time I went to an Institute for Alcoholism, but went right back into drinking. It became more than I could handle. My work was slowing down because of the booze. I was getting tired—wearing down. My mind was foggier all the time. Sometimes drugs were also involved, but mainly it was drinking from early morning to late at night.

All this time I thought of the Lord, but the obsession for making money was greater. There is nothing wrong with success, but in seeking for it, I forsook my loyalty to Christ. Sometimes I would sober up long enough to see the condition that I was in. I would say to myself—"Don't you realize what you are doing to yourself? You know that Jesus Christ is coming back someday—you are responsible for everything that you do!"

The guilt was there all the time, and I would drink to get away from it. There were few sober times during all those years. I would even wake up in the middle of the night

sometimes to get a drink. It was ridiculous.

I caused my family embarrassment and trouble. I became very inconsiderate, hurting people—mainly my family. It was getting to the point that my temper was becoming violent.

I know what it means to be completely destitute and empty on the inside. There were all kinds of "things" on the outside, but all of the successes—bigger cars, bigger houses, more expensive wines, more pictures on the walls, bigger boats, softer beds—the things people consider to be "success"—they were all temporary. Didn't last long. I would go out to my boat on the lake trying to enjoy myself, all the time knowing that Jesus was Lord—that I would someday answer to Him for the things I had done.

I was totally miserable: having Christ in my heart, yet living with my face set against Him. It was like being a slave, in bondage to alcohol.

The last few months of 1975 saw Dallas afraid of turning back to the Lord for fear of losing his star-studded songwriting career, yet in a hellish enigma of DT's and empty bottles and guilt-filled wooziness. Finally, he made a trip to Gatlinburg to sort out the problems. Something had to be done. Dallas knew it. Sharon longed for it. As Dallas spent many hours in desperation in the motel room, back at home Sharon claimed God's promises; she and the three girls knelt many times tearfully asking God to deliver their daddy from the bondage that had made their home into a hell.

I had gone away several times to ask the Lord to help me. I knew that He could deliver me from alcohol, but I also knew that you had to do your part in getting away from it. You know, alcohol is very deceiving—you can think up a thousand different reasons for drinking, good reasons if you need a drink.

I never dreamed that I would get as low as I did. I was even put in jail four times during the years, once in California. But I went to Gatlinburg with the sincere desire to give it up. During the last few months of 1975, Sharon and I had gotten a lot closer—I knew that I had to straighten up and she sensed my sincerity.

I went up to Gatlinburg a few days before New Year's Eve. I still kept some liquor in my room, but was seeking the Lord's help. God began moving, and on the third of January, I had gotten rid of the booze and went through the whole day without drinking. It wasn't easy. It had been a long, long time since that had happened.

This time it was no accident; God had begun a miracle—a work of such magnitude and power to bring a man out of a seemingly endless and unquenchable habit.

Jesus said . . . , "I am the resurrection, and the life, he that believeth in me, though he were dead, yet shall he live" (John 11:25).

Driving back toward home that night of the third, Dallas began to talk with the Lord about his past, confessing the things he did. It was a special never-to-be-forgotten time.

I poured my heart out to Him. I remember praying—"Lord, if my life is like a big blackboard, then please just take Your eraser and erase all my sins and failures. Let me start with a clean slate tonight!"

I felt forgiven! Though the devil has fought me every inch of the way since then, I knew that night that I had a joy within me that I hadn't had for ages—fourteen or fifteen years.

A new husband came home to Sharon that night. Melody, Robin, and Alison welcomed back a new daddy. Dallas came back home with a newfound love for the Lord, his family, and God's Word.

I didn't know where to start with the thousands of things to catch up on. I wanted to study the Word of God. I wanted to fellowship with Christians.

I went to a Bible bookstore, and was amazed at all the books and new translations and study helps on the market. I had been so far away from those things that I didn't know what was going on.

I was so thirsty to learn. One day I went in and spent $200 on commentaries and dictionaries and books. I wanted to get started in the Word of God. Our family started studying the Bible TOGETHER and going to church regularly TOGETHER.

Sharon's so happy. It's a different life. We've had more of a life together and shared more since then than in all the time before. The girls had been Christians for some time. They're pretty happy now because they knew that their dad was in quite a bit of trouble. It's been a whole new life for all of us.

Life is simpler now. The glitter and sham has been exchanged with a comfortable but not-lavish home near Gallatin. The farm isn't filled with famous friends and clinking glasses of bourbon; the church they attend isn't as luxurious as the night spots Dallas used to frequent in Music City; waiting on the Lord for guidance and direction and power isn't near as "successful" as writing number one songs (although that may return someday too), but Dallas Frazier has a whole new outlook about many things, especially success.

Many people associate success with things, but you have to be successful in your own inner being before you can really know happiness or "success." I believe that any person who knows Jesus Christ as his personal Saviour knows this; those who don't are still looking for it. I can sympathize with them—I know what it means to have all kinds of things on the outside and yet be completely empty and destitute on the inside.

Though he tried and tried to outrun the God who loved him; though he tried to get past the prayers of the family who loved him—he simply failed. In failing, he finally succeeded. Faith and prayer and God's power are still stronger than "things."

Welcome home, Dallas Frazier.

LARRY GATLIN—SINGER, SONGWRITER
**Grammy Award-winning singer and songwriter—
"Broken Lady," "Help Me," "If Practice Makes Perfect"**

He steps into the spotlight. After the boisterous applause fades, he sits on the ever-present wooden stool. There's an expectant hush, then skilled fingers strum silver guitar strings.

He begins to sing, "I don't wanna cry this early this morning . . .

More cheering.

Out in the audience, strangers grin at each other—this is what they came to hear. Their singer is no "Outlaw," no rhinestone personality. Larry Gatlin wears faded jeans that somehow seem genuine. That's it—genuine; that's what the people came to hear.

Song after song, the audience feels the soul-deep stirring beneath the harmonies. More poet than songwriter; more song painter than singer, Larry Gatlin is one of the most unique and successful young troubadours in the country.

Today, he is one of the most sought-after country artists in the business, both for his singing and songwriting. His songs are being increasingly recorded by the giants of the music industry. His shining Grammy Award will no doubt soon be joined by others. His concerts are regularly jammed with admirers. He has even started to catch jabs from psuedo-critics—a sure sign of success.

It hasn't always been this together for Larry Gatlin; though his story isn't filled with horrible sins-to-salvation or rags-to-riches, it is still a tribute to the unmistakable working of God.

Larry Gatlin entered the world in Seminole, Texas (also the birth-place of Tanya Tucker). His dad kept "beans and 'taters" on the table by working as a driller in west Texas oilfields. Larry's childhood was normal with nothing out of the ordinary, except for a lifelong love affair with music.

When I was about four, my parents were asked by some friends who were big Gospel music fans to go to a large Gospel singing in Abilene. They tried to leave me home, but there aren't many four-year-olds who like to stay at home when their parents are going out, so they took me along. I remember that it was at the Fair Park Auditorium next to the zoo.

The Blackwood Brothers and the Statesmen were singing that night. Wow! I fell in love with it—the music was exciting. I was just a little kid, but I went nuts over how good it sounded. It was my first real experience with music, and I guess that's why Gospel music is still my first love.

At that first concert, his parents bought several of the 78 rpm recordings from the singers, recordings that were to greatly influence Larry and his two younger brothers. *I loved 'em. We played 'em all the time—singing along—learning the words.*

When Larry was six years old, his mother entered him in a talent contest held as a preliminary to a Blackwood Brothers-Statesmen concert.

My Aunt Nellie told my mother to let my two brothers (Steve was four years old and Rudy was only two and half) to "let 'em all three sing!" then Aunt Nellie told the promoters of the talent contest "My three nephews can out-sing the Blackwood Brothers AND Jake Hess." She never was one at a loss for words!

Rudy was so little that they stood him up on a Dr. Pepper crate. We got up there and sang "Angels Watching Over Me." We had learned it from the 78's—Rudy and Steve sang lead and I sang Bill Shaw's tenor part.

Not only did the audience go crazy at these three little boys singing a Blackwood Brothers' song, but to top it off—Rudy fell off the Dr. Pepper box on the last note. That really tore 'em down!!

That was not only the first singing experience for the three, but soon led to more singing engagements—eventually all over America.

Mom and Dad were really wise. They wanted to keep our childhood normal. We went to school, played sports, sang in the church choir, just like any other kid on the block. The only other time it was different for us was during summers and on weekends when we would travel and sing. We made a bunch of little albums on the Sword and Shield Records in Arlington.

The musical career ended temporarily when Larry accepted a football scholarship to the University of Houston.

I played thirteen whole minutes in three years behind two All-Americans—Kenny Hebert and Elmo Wright. Actually, I did play first-string during pre-season one year at halfback in front of Cliff Branch and Elmo Wright for one week until the coaches finally figured out that both of them could run faster backwards than I could frontwards!

After graduation from the University, Larry entered law school, supposedly saying good-bye to music. Soon, however, that first love once again stirred.

I called Lari Goss in Atlanta about a demo tape I had sent to him. During the conversation he told me that the Imperials were looking for a baritone.

After talking with Lari Goss, Larry called Armond Morales whom he had known when Armond traveled through the Midwest and Southwest with the Weatherfords. Armond and the Imperials *were* looking for a baritone and were backing Elvis Presley in Las Vegas, and asked Larry to come and try out with them in Vegas.

Excitedly, Larry packed away his dreams for becoming a lawyer with his Blackstone books (ironically, Blackstone, the famous judge whose commentaries are study-standards for law students, actually wanted to be a poet). As he said farewell to law school, Larry Gatlin—singer-writer-poet reemerged.

We finished the schedule with Elvis, then worked with Jimmy Dean. After closing with Jimmy, I went back home to Houston to wait and see if I had gotten the job with the Imperials. It seemed that my dream of singing with a professional quartet was coming true.

Not long afterwards, they called me back—said they had not yet made up their mind and could I come join them at the Landmark Hotel where they were to back up Jimmy Dean?

As it worked out, they eventually hired Greg Gordon instead of me, but while I was in Vegas, I met Dottie West. One night there was a bunch of us in one of the rooms offstage talking and singing. I picked up Dottie's new Ovation guitar and started singing one of my songs. I had written some songs by then, but I let her think that I was making the words up as I sang.

She said—"You're making that up aren't you? That's pretty good. Actually, you look enough like Mickey Newberry that you oughta be a writer."

Before I left Las Vegas, she asked me to send her a tape of some of my songs. When I got back to Houston, my wife borrowed a Wollensack tape recorder from the school where she was teaching. I quickly recorded eight songs that I had written by then. It wasn't long until Dottie sent me a plane ticket to Nashville.

With his Texas grin, Larry still gives much of the credit for his success to Miss West. *"If it hadn't been for Dottie, who knows—I would probably be a world famous criminal attorney in Houston by now!"*

Though his first year in Nashville was less than illustrous, it was a genuine foundation for later victorious years. His wife began teaching school in the Nashville system; Larry got a job at WLAC sweeping floors and moving props.

We were very fortunate. We never starved since both of us went right to work. A lot of songwriters come to Nashville acting like a cloak from heaven has just fallen on them; they just hang around playing pinball and drinking beer waiting for the inspiration to fall in the form of hit songs. That's a bunch of hogwash—a man's first obligation is to pay his bills and take care of his family.

I hung around some and met a lot of people when I got there—people like Mickey Newberry, Jeannie Seely, and Hank Cockran—but could never see just sitting around waiting for something to happen like so many of the young writers. So, I went to work.

Dottie still had my tape, plus Rudy and Steve (then students at Texas Tech) had come to Nashville during a break and had cut another demo tape in Dottie's living room.

Dottie told Kris Kristofferson about the tape earlier, and not long after she told him we were at the studio watching Kris record. He called out to Dottie—"Hey, West—you still got that tape of that kid from Texas?"

I practically flew to my house, got the tape, went back to the studio. Kris and Fred Foster (president of Monument Records) both heard it. They liked the songs, and the rest is history.

That break was exactly what he needed. A recording contract with Monument was soon signed. Also, it wasn't long until many well-known artists began using his material. Actually, the very first song Larry had recorded was by Dottie West—"You're The Other Half Of Me."

It was like getting in the major leagues and getting your first base hit. My first song wasn't a big hit—if it had been, it would have been like a home run on your first bat.

As Larry became better known in Nashville, he and Kristofferson crossed paths often. Kris obviously left an indelible mark.

Kris was kind of my guiding light. He is a beautiful person. It's a pity that though I was a born-again Christian all during the time I hung out with Kris and the rest of his crowd, I wasn't helping him because I was doing the same things they were. I never was a very good influence around him; I never was the kind of Christian witness that I should have been. Still, I do know that Kris is the most decent, honest human being I've ever known.

Being a Christian hasn't always been popular or easy as it seems to be today, especially for those in the public eye.

It's never been fashionable to humble yourself before God. I'm not trying to water down the times that I failed Him. I'm a human being that makes mistakes, and even though I've done many wrong things, His grace has always been sufficient.

I have no doubt that God has had His hand on me since childhood, and I'm thankful for what He's allowed me to accomplish. I accepted Him when I was a kid, and He's been with me ever since.

Just as his life is genuine, so has been his constant climb to the top of the song-writing ladder. Some of his biggest songs include "Delta Dirt"—a top ten Country-Western hit in 1974; "Help Me"—a song written especially for Kris Kristofferson with big hits recorded by Elvis Presley, the Oak Ridge Boys and others; "Statues Without Hearts"—a top rated C & W chart climber; "If Practice Makes Perfect"—a giant sung by Johnny Rodriquez; "I Don't Wanna Cry" a top ten chart buster; "Broken Lady"—the Grammy Award-winning Best Country Song of 1977; and the gospel classic "Light At The End Of The Darkness."

1978 was Larry Gatin's greatest year yet with multi-awards, numerous chart hits: "Love Is Just A Game," "Anything But Leavin'," "I Just Wish You Were Someone I Love," and "Night Time Magic." These songs were born from deep emotions and a love for the language, so there are stories behind many of the lyrics. Since then Larry has been honored, applauded, and exalted. Clearly the Gatlin pen and sound will continue to cause classic excitement with each new hit.

"I Don't Wanna Cry": I was at an Atlanta radio station. We came in and the DJ jokingly told me that he didn't want me to tell any sad stories because it was too early to cry. BOOINNGG! I went into the restroom, away from the rest of the people, and wrote the song in just a few minutes.

"Broken Lady": I had gone through a dry period in 1976. I kept trying writing different things but nothing worked. Fred Foster stood by me even though I wasn't getting any record action. I even cut some material written by other writers but it wasn't where I was at so it didn't come out very good.

Finally, I went to Chicago to do a show with Tex Davis, record producer for Monument Records. Afterwards, as I watched Ramsey Lewis do his part of the show, suddenly the thought hit me—"You idiot! You're supposed to be a hit songwriter. Quit moping around and write a hit song."

I wrote "Broken Lady" in twenty minutes on the way home from the airport, and felt from the first that it was a hit. I tried it out on my wife, then did it at the Exit/Inn Showcase in Nashville. They loved it. Not long after I recorded it, it went to number one nationally, and February, 1977, won the Grammy. Needless to say, I was pretty surprised that it won over Waylon and Willie's songs.

"Light At The End Of The Darkness": I was playing rhythm for one of Johnny Cash's recording sessions. After taping one evening, he said "Pilgrim, why don't you write me

*a pop-inspirational-type song. Not a 'Gone-to-Heaven-in Eb'
thing, but a song that shows people how I really feel about the
Lord."*

*I told John that I would. I decided to take my time and plan
and mechanically do what I usually do spontaneously, but
what actually happened is that I got the idea for "Light"
about halfway home from the session in Hendersonville. It
took me about seven minutes to write it.*

Several recording artist have had giant hits with the
song—it was a great cut on the Imperial's "No Shortage"
album—a Grammy Award winner in 1976. But that was just
the beginning of this classic inspirational song.

*I've had lot of people write—"If it wasn't for that song, I
couldn't get along."*

*There's also a strange story connected to the song. The day
Freddie Prinze ("Chico and the Man"—TV program) shot
himself, I had to do a TV talk show. He was still alive for part
of the day, but I hadn't even heard about his suicide; I had
just got up in time to go to the studio for the "Nashville Noon
Show."*

*I did "Statues Without Hearts," then Teddy Bart, the host
of the program, said "Here's a song I wish Freddie Prinze
could have heard before he died," and I sang "Light At The
End Of The Darkness."*

*Afterwards, I packed up my guitar and left the studio. I
went to the Friday night Opry, and Tex Davis came up to me
all excited. I asked, "Are you all right?"*

*He said, "I've got to tell you something!" Then he related a
bizarre story about a young lady—twenty-three or twenty-
four years old—who had awakened the morning of Freddie
Prinze's suicide, heard about it on the radio. He was her
favorite actor. She really loved him, but went to work though
blue and despondent. When she got to work, she found that
she had been fired.*

She said "That's it! I'm giving up on all this mess. If Fred-

die can't even make it with all his success, I'm not going to try any more."

On the way home, she got a bottle of prescription sleeping pills and went back to the apartment—still planning to do the big number.

Her roommate had left the TV on—the "Noon Show" was on the air and Teddy Bart was announcing that Larry Gatlin was going to be on the show. She decided to watch her favorite singer on the show before killing herself. After I sang "Light At The End Of The Darkness," she flushed the pills down the toilet!!

Something like that reinforces my belief that what I'm doing is right. I don't believe that I'm anything special, but if the songs I write help to save somebody and get them started on the right road—that's worth it all.

It's also humbling to think that if I had sung something about drinking or cheating, that girl would have been dead that day.

The songs and the stories are real, like the writer. He is refreshingly unusual and original in a too-often-stale industry. Moreover, being a genuine Christian in an industry not-so-genuine and not-so-Christian must surely pose problems, especially to a man like Larry who accepted the Lord as his Saviour as a child and was raised in a church.

It gets to me. It would get to anyone who opens up his life for all the public to see; yet it hasn't been impossible.

Something really special happened to me last year that helped my spiritual life tremendously. I was playing at the Troubadour in Las Vegas. Chuck Woolery, best-known for being host on TV's "Wheel of Fortune," was also there opening for Dan and Dick (of "Laugh-In" fame). He saw me and asked me to come by his room to talk.

Chuck is a real turned-on Christian; he said "You're troubled—I can tell."

I was. "Well—it's a long road." He kind of looked inside me and saw that I was trying to be all things to all men. "You're feeling guilty of maybe failing somebody and it's eating you up. You know the Bible says in Romans 8:1, 'There is therefore no condemnation to them which are in Christ Jesus, who walk not after the flesh, but after the Spirit.' "

He explained that I should let this knowledge creep down from my head to my heart. What he shared with me has been a real help. It's been a whole new ball game since then. I'm just me—any place or time. I can praise God and thank Him for that place or time. I don't have to gripe or complain if others have hit records. If it's not my time, I'll stay at home—write songs, play golf, spend time with my family.

I can't be all things to all men—I have to be me, exactly what God made me to be. I was mad at the world before, but now I see my purpose. I'm not Oral Roberts or Billy Graham. I just try to paint pictures of life as I see it. I know I'm doing what I should be doing. Everything kind of springs from that.

His main purpose obviously is to write and sing special songs, something so many try but so few succeed in doing.

Everybody wants to write songs—they think it's so easy. To try to write hit songs day in and day out is hard work.

Everybody can't be firemen or a brain surgeon or a mailman; likewise, everybody can't be a songwriter just because they want to be.

If I couldn't write songs, I'd pack up and go home and get a job.

But Larry does write, well enough to win Grammy and Country Music Association awards. His songs continue to be among the top-rated all across the nation. "I've Done Enough Dying Today," and other glittering 1979 efforts are just promises of what is to come during the new decade. There is an obvious difference in the quality of his songs.

I try to make my lyrics meaningful—not trite—"she left me—I'm so blue—I gotta get drunk"-type stuff. This is different from a lot of people. The masses like trite or general music so that's what most of the successful writers give 'em, but to me—it's not enough just to entertain people.

69

Somehow that straight-ahead philosophy spills over to all areas of Larry's life.

When I started out, I wanted to be the biggest star in the world, but that's not important any more. I have a new goal—I'm looking for a hundred places in America where I can go work for three to five thousand people. If you get over that number, the accoustics are terrible and they can't hear the lyrics, which is what I want 'em to hear.

It's great to know that the people come to see Larry Gatlin and his band, and it's nice to hear their applause and get standing ovations, but I'd rather have the people remember the lyrics.

I just want to be what I'm supposed to be. I don't want Neil Diamond's or Peter Frampton's or Kris Kristofferson's place.

It's not hard to notice that Larry Gatlin's music goes far beneath the surface lyrics.

I write songs like I see life. I'm just one normal, Joe Blow, everyday person, and I tell people how I see it. They can either say "Yes, I agree" and like it, or "No, I don't agree." I'm not gonna preach.

For so long preachers have tried to tell people how they ought to act, which is okay and something that's needed, but the real decisions have to come from the inside out—not just because somebody tells them what to do.

I just tell'em how it is—then let them make the changes. Songs like "Help Me" and "Light At The End Of The Darkness" tell the best way as I see it. I get letters everyday from people who have been touched and changed, so it seems to be working.

Larry Gatlin is unique in his genunineness. His world revolves around simplicity and reality. Some ancient sage once wrote, "Simplicity is the highest form of elegance." Solid things are important to him: The Lord, his music, and his family. Larry quips that his lovely wife, Janis, is "much too good for this cowboy"; Kristin, their daughter and Joshua Cash, their son; and his traveling band, a finally-fulfilled dream to travel again with his brothers, Steve and Rudy.

His life is a nonstop succession of recording sessions, one-nighters on the road, long-awaited moments at home, appearances at the Grand Ole Opry (said by many to be the most exciting hit there in years), television tapings, including a multi-televised commercial for a national telephone company, lists of awards, songs written in dog-eared notebooks, and an endless variety of roads and jet streams. All of it is motivated by a man with a God-given purpose to communicate his life through songs.

Whatever he does, whatever tomorrow holds, it is bound to be honest and legitimate. Genuine, like Larry Gatlin.

CONNIE SMITH HAYNES—
SUCCESSFUL OVERNIGHT BUT NOT HAPPY

**Top country songstress—"Once A Day," "Just One Time,"
"I Just Want to Be Your Everything!"**

Photo: Billy Deaton Talent

There are few stories of sudden storybook success in the
music industry that are really true. "Instant stardom" has
usually taken years of struggling for that "big break."

Connie Smith ranks as one of America's true overnight
country music successes. Approximately a year spanned the
time from the day she won a talent contest (that she reluc-
tantly entered) where Bill Anderson discovered her, to the
phenomenonal moment when her first recording, "Once A
Day," became a number one country hit.

It was an incredible, whirlwind spiral, but this is only part
of the real "Connie Smith Story." Though the next few years
would see many more top records and spreading fame, it

72

would also bring a crushing crescendo of problems falling full force on Connie's young shoulders. Permanent relief was to be light-years away.

Connie was born in Elkhart, Indiana. When she was five months old, her parents moved to West Virginia. Her blood father unfortunately was a slave to alcohol and when under the influence of it, frequently mistreated his wife and five children, so Connie's mother eventually had no choice but to leave him. A year after the divorce, a "Brady Bunch"-type story evolved.

My oldest sister was a young teenager when she met this boy at school the same age, whose father no longer had a wife, but did have eight children he was raising alone. Through those two kids meeting (they later married and had five children) my mother and his father met and soon married, later adding a little girl of their own to the already oversized family.

Connie and all the "brood of youngins" moved all over the southeastern Ohio area. Her stepdad was an itinerant carpenter, sharecropper, heavy equipment operator— anything to feed the sixteen hungry mouths. The kids pitched in by scrounging through the woods for ginseng and sassafras to sell. The conglomeration alleviated the dire poverty by raising their own food. Everyone grew up fast—out of necessity. Connie still vividly remembers the houses with no window glass, torturously cold during the long, Ohio winters, and irritating during the regular invasion of flies and insects every summer.

One temporary relief came through the radio. It brought laughter and news and a bit of the sunshiny outside into their poverty. It also brought music.

My interest in music started 'way back then. My real daddy was an Ernest Tubb fan—really big on him. When we had a radio, my stepdad listened to the Grand Ole Opry every Saturday night.

Always with a flip, so that no one could tell she was really

73

revealing her dream, she would quip, even as a five-year-old, "I'm gonna be on the Grand Ole Opry someday."

But the real world then was a world of poverty. Being extremely poor does one of two things: it can bury any flicker of hope, or it can ignite a desire to pull one's self up life's ladder. For Connie—the ember refused to be extinguished, though there were many reasons for it to be.

We moved around a lot, always looking for something better. I attended eight different schools, finally graduating from Salem-Liberty High School in Lower Salem, Ohio.

Connie was salutatorian of her senior class, though she remarks today, "Then I must've outgrown that!"

That senior year held more than academic honors; however, another career began, a result of unusual circumstances.

I was supposed to go to the high school prom. One of my older sisters had worked and gotten enough money to order a $16 formal—a white one with a red rose and all like they used to be, through the mail order catalog, most of our clothing were what someone had given us. Anyway, she gave it to me and I couldn't wait to wear it to the senior prom. Well, before the prom we moved, and in the process of moving, someone stole a lot of things out of the house, the formal among them, so when it came time for the prom, I was too embarrassed to go in a regular skirt and blouse so I told everybody that I didn't want to go to the dumb old prom. So, I went to the square dance instead, in my skirt and blouse.

Some of the people at the dance knew I sang with my brother and sister in church, so they asked me to come up and sing. I got $3 for singing that night.

That was quite an eventful night, for another dream, just as longstanding, was on its way to being fulfilled. The handsome young brown-haired guy I met at that dance, named Jerry Smith, would, a couple of years later, give me the name that would be well-know in that budding singing career, and much more important, give me my first-born son.

From the less-than-illustrious beginning, that initial, impromptu performance led to other "bookings" at local PTA and Grange meetings. Then came a small break.

That year at our county fair, a group of singers came to perform. They had been on the air at WSAZ in Huntington, West Virginia, for ten years doing the "Saturday Night Jamboree" live every week.

Somebody told them that I could sing. They thought that it would be good to include some local talent on the program, so they asked me to sing a couple of songs.

I'd been married about a year, four months pregnant, and scared to death, but I sang "Honky Tonk Angels" and "Pick Me Up On Your Way Down." The square dancers were waiting to come on stage after I finished and as I started to leave the stage, they all stepped back and were applauding. I thought that they were just scooting out of the way so I could get off the stage, but later someone told me they were leading the audience in a standing ovation.

A few months later, the group from WSAZ contacted Connie. Their girl singer who had been with them for ten years had left, and they were holding a contest to fill her position. Connie won the contest and sang regularly each Saturday night on the "Jamboree" for several months until another storybook occurrence.

I had never been to the Grand Ole Opry, but we heard about a park in Columbus, Ohio, that featured many of the Opry stars. Friends of ours told us that George Jones was going to be there on a certain day. He was my favorite singer so we went down to hear him. What happened was that we had been given the wrong schedule. Bill Anderson was there instead.

They had a talent contest there every Sunday, and since we were there anyway, our friends talked me into entering. I was scared—not so much of singing, but I was pretty proud, and was mainly afraid that I wouldn't win.

She did enter. She won. She not only collected the five shiny silver dollars as a prize but got to meet "Whisperin' " Bill in person. To top the other excitement, she was featured that night in Anderson's show.

A few months later—Connie and Jerry (by then the proud parents of a baby boy), went to another Bill Anderson concert. He recognized them, took them to dinner, asked Connie to come to Nashville to audition some material he had written, and booked her to perform on Ernest Tubb's Record Shop radio show in March of '64.

Chet Atkins heard the demo tape she made for Bill and immediately signed her to an exclusive recording contract with RCA in 1964. She has always wanted to make a record—this childlike wish became an unbelievable reality. Her first recording, "Once A Day," zoomed to the number one slot on charts across the nation. Connie Smith literally became a full-fledged overnight star.

Along with the instant success came the first financial benefits, something she had never before experienced. Her first "spending sprees" were not extravagant flings on jewelry, autos, or houses; instead, she bought items that exhibited the deep degree of poverty she had seen before.

All my life I had never had a lot. I remember always wanting to have all the milk I could drink, or real grapes from the grocery store. To me, that was being rich.

Another thing, I used to look at the catalogs and dream of being able to someday have all the clothes that I was wearing at ONE time to all be new. They didn't have to be expensive or anything, but just all new at one time together.

When I came to Nashville, I didn't want to be rich or famous. I guess even then all I wanted was to be married and have a bunch of kids and have a happy home.

Sadly, happiness remained an unreachable wish, though fame continued to fling its sparkling spotlight on Connie's beautiful portrait. Two more Bill Anderson tunes—"I Can't Remember" and "Tiny Blue Transistor" reached the top ten on most national charts. In 1967, "Ain't Had No Lovin'," written by Dallas Frazier, was another top hit. Again and again during the following years, her songs were to spiral to the public pinnacle. Thousands and thousands of her single and album recordings were sold. DJ's continued to spin her popular discs. Her fame grew as she sang on numerous one-nighter tours across the nation. Life could have never been more beautiful. Or was it?

I had always wanted these things, and all of a sudden I had so many things that I had wished for, but I still wasn't happy.

I was married, but I wasn't happy. My first marriage ended. I was very immature. I was seeking a god instead of a husband—it was that simple. I figured that when I got married that everything would work out.

I think one reason marriages fail is because so many women—maybe men too—make their mate a god; then, if he's not always understanding, not always forgiving, not always there—in other words—if he's not always perfect, then everything falls apart.

With my first record a hit, we came to Nashville and bought a home. Our life style changed drastically, still these things didn't bring the happiness I expected.

I got to be part of the Grand Ole Opry (a regular member since 1965), but that didn't make me happy.

All these things—the records, the home, marriage, success, clothes—all these things that as a kid I thought would make me happy—the more I got of 'em, the more unhappy I became.

Within a year after her first marriage broke up, she was again wed, this time to Jack Watkins, an exceptional guitarist in Nashville. Once again, she was an insecure girl looking for the storybook hero who would make her live happily ever after. Once again, failure.

She sought answers. She saw psychiatrists weekly. Nothing helped. She didn't try pills or alcohol as an out simply because she had a vivid memory of the effect on her father. She went to church off and on, but she couldn't keep from crying and was too proud to let people see her openly weeping. She had never heard of the conviction that the Holy Spirit gives to needy hearts. She had attended church before but didn't know that people had to be "saved" through Jesus Christ or they would be lost in their nonaction and unbelief. She had been "religious," at eighteen, having gone through a nervous breakdown trying to get "good enough" to "feel" she would qualify for heaven. Trying this in her own strength only resulted in failure. *At that time, I wasn't aware that it is God looking at us through the shed blood of Jesus Christ when we have accepted Him as our Saviour that makes us acceptable in His eyes. The righteousness of Christ then becomes our righteousness and we receive this through faith in Him—this is what brings the true peace that I was searching for in my life.*

In April 1968, Jimmy Snow asked me to do a Gospel song on WSM's "Gospel Country" show. I always did a hymn on my country show, but when I started singing on his program, I started crying.

She sang "In The Garden," then sat down out of camera range as Jimmy finished the telecast. What a contrast of ironies—the striking blonde singer with numerous top national awards, including a recent "Female Vocalist of the Year" laurel, sitting with warm tears flowing down her grief-striken face. At twenty-six, Connie Smith had everything her heart could possibly desire—except for the most important Thing.

Jimmy Snow finished the program and came to talk with his guest singer. He knew what was happening.

I didn't know why I was crying. I had never heard much about the Holy Spirit. I wasn't aware of a personal saving God. If I had heard about it in church as a child, I just didn't remember.

Deep down, I didn't think anybody loved me. I had a good mama, but I was one of fourteen kids so there wasn't a lot of time for her to show me attention and love.

As a kid, I couldn't run or jump well, so I was just real lonesome. I had always been a "people watcher."

That night in 1968, Connie Smith stopped being a "people

watcher." As the cameramen, band, and studio audience looked on, Jimmy Snow shared verses that proved God's love for her. After the show, Jimmy sat outside the studio in Connie's new Cadillac and led her in the sinner's prayer.

I didn't feel real sure of my salvation for the first year, but I hung onto His Word that said if I would ask Him inside, He WOULD come in. I went forward for every altar call for awhile to make sure I was saved. Finally, the Holy Spirit showed me that I was still trying to work for my salvation instead of just accepting His finished work on the cross.

Actually, the assurance came when I went with some friends to hear Rev. Doyle Jennings, who was holding a revival. People were praying for the baptism of the Holy Spirit. I had prayed for "It" before, but didn't receive "It" so I felt I wasn't good enough.

That night at the revival, people began praying all around me. I wasn't used to everyone praying aloud in a service. The two ladies on either side of me were praying so loud that I couldn't concentrate. Finally, to block them out, I started saying "Thank You, Jesus." Suddenly, it hit me that I was speaking in tongues. Here, after all this time of asking the Lord for the baptism, I received the gift, when I wasn't even thinking or praying for it. It was just the beautiful way of God, because I didn't get it in my own way. From that time on, I had the assurance of my salvation.

I learned to stay in His Word even when I didn't understand or feel anything, because His Word always remains faithful.

What a difference! Connie Smith now lives with that captivating smile that has replaced the inward insecurities. Her bubbling personality is only matched by a desire to see others come to the same Person who has changed her so dramatically. She's not ashamed to proclaim her new Master publicly—either through her songs or through her spoken heart-outpouring. She appears frequently on television programs and crusades with David Wilkerson, Billy Graham,

James Robison, Rex and Maude Aimee Humbard.

Since the world still thinks that becoming a Christian means instant public failure, Connie continues to reverse stereotypes. Her records continue to sell at a furious clip. Almost every single she's released has reached the top ten national charts. In 1969, she struck with "Ribbon of Darkness." "Where Is My Castle" (written by Dallas Frazier) was a giant 1971 song. She posted another number one classic in 1972 with Don Gibson's "Just One Time." Another Frazier tune—"If It Ain't Love (Let's Leave It Alone)" hit in 1973. Two more of Dallas's songs broke in 1974—"Ain't Had No Lovin' " and "Ain't Love A Good Thing." She struck again in the top five with Don Everly's "Till I Kissed You" in 1976.

Then Connie inked a contract with Monument Records; the results were once again riding the top rated listings. 1978's biggest was the top ten hit, "I Just Want To Be Your Everything."

When I signed with Fred Foster (President of Monument), I prayed for the Lord NOT to give me a hit record unless He wanted it. A big song means more money, but it's not worth it unless it's in His perfect will, for with it comes increased responsibility and pressure from the world to concentrate on self and frustration from not being allowed to solely lift up Jesus.

God has graciously supplied me with wholesome country songs throughout my career, but I have cried to the Lord many times in the past few years, that although I love country music, I no longer need the satisfaction of a career. I long to sing only when the emphasis is solely on Him and His Word and to share His love and the victory He has brought into my life and into the lives of many of those I love. Not long ago, through a dream the Lord gave me, I received a peace that I had been searching for concerning this. God assured me that He knows how I feel and that it is all in His hands and His time. I thank God for His peace that passes all our understanding!

Connie's growing family places increasing demands upon her time, although she continues making records, doing a limited amount of personal appearances throughout the world each month, singing and hosting on numerous television shows, and performing regularly on the Grand Ole Opry. However, with constant prayer and guidance from the Lord, her family still receives most of her attention.

She is married to Marshall Haynes, whose testimony is equally touching and exciting. God brought him out of a self-life, including a broken marriage, drug addiction, alcohol, etc. Together, Marshall and Connie have five vibrant children, two boys and three girls, ranging from toddler to teen age. God has pieced together a collection of miracles that today stands as a monumental reminder of His healing ability.

Except for Connie's brief visits to the public eye, the Haynes live "everyday" lives. Connie keeps the awards and momentos closeted. Marshall works as a muscled and T-shirted Western Electric employee. Their days are completely ordinary. Darren, the eldest boy, mows the lawn. His younger brother, Kerry, has a new baseball cap and doesn't think too much of this author's being a Dodger fan. The two oldest girls, Julie and Jeanne, play with dolls, and the youngest girl, Jodie, shows an artistic inclination with a pencil on my notebook as I try to write. On Sundays, the family attends the Lord's Chapel, where Marshall teaches an adult Sunday school class.

In other words, they appear to be a typical family, despite Connie's sparkling fame. More than anything else, Connie and Marshall and the children are beautiful examples of what God can do even in the face of impossible odds. Jesus said that the things which are "impossible with men are possible with God" (Luke 18:27).

Connie Smith continues to be tradition's opposite. Just as she was an overnight success when instant fame was a myth, so now she is anything but a stereotyped star. She consciously lets God control her steps, saying, "My career is not guided by shows or records anymore." In fact, when accepting the recent thirteenth Annual Music News Country Award for "Best Gospel Act," she expressed a new trend for her life. "I'm not really a gospel act, but I love the Lord. He sure is good to me. In a way this is a confirmation. I've just recorded my last country album and just did my last country concert. I'll just be doing gospel from now on."

Though the oft-typed role of singing idol is that of an obnoxious, worried, arrogant person, Connie is a curious montage of smiles and warmth and originality. Though public stardom supposedly rules out a happy family role, her family not only comes first but is constantly growing closer because God is the acknowledged Head.

Many "overnight successes," like matchbook lights, flare and die in an instant. For Connie Smith, the flame lives; only the fuel has changed.

"For it is God which worketh in you both to will and to do of his good pleasure . . . [to be] blameless and harmless, the sons [daughters] of God, without rebuke, in the midst of a crooked and perverse nation, among whom ye shine as lights in the world; holding forth the word of life; that I may rejoice in the day of Christ, that I have not run in vain, neither labored in vain" (Phil. 2:13, 15-16).

JOHN D. LOUDERMILK—
AWAY FROM THE CITY, BACK TO THE LORD
Hall of Fame songwriter—"Ebony Eyes," "Talk Back Trembling Lips," "Indian Reservation," "Break My Mind"

1971. LaFayette, Louisiana. A thirty-eight-year-old man, his wife, and their three sons came into town. They had no family or friends there—no connections at all. Without fanfare or explanation, they moved into a big old cypress house on St. Francis Street, owned formerly by a history professor.

Naturally, townspeople wondered where he came from and why he had no regular job like other people. Some suggested that he might have just retired early. Maybe a secret CIA agent?

Little did they know that the distinguished-looking man was one of the most successful songwriters in the history of recorded music. His catalog of recorded songs read like a treasury of all-time hits.

"Rose And A Baby Ruth"—1957—#1 pop and coun-
    try—George Hamilton IV
"Waterloo"—#1 pop and country—Stonewall Jackson
"Amigo's Guitar"—1960—#1 country—Kitty Wells
"Grin and Bear It"—1960—top 10 country and pop—Jimmy
    C. Newman
"Ebony Eyes"—1961—#1—Everly Brothers
"Sad Movies Make Me Cry"—1961—#1 pop and country—
    Sue Thompson
"Thou Shalt Not Steal"—1962—top five pop—
    Dick and Dee Dee
"Norman"—1962—#1—Sue Thompson
"Abilene"—1963—#1 pop and country—George Hamilton IV
"Talk Back Trembling Lips"—1963—#1 country—
    Ernie Ashworth, #1 pop—Johnny Tillotson
"Bad News"—1964—top 10 country—Johnny Cash
    and Doug Kershaw
"Tobacco Road"—1964—#1 pop in America & England—
    Nashville Teens and Edgar Winter
"Sitting In The Balcony"—1965—top five pop—
    Eddie Cochran
"Then You Can Tell Me Good-bye"—1967—#1 pop—Casinos
    1969—#1 country—Eddie Arnold
"Break My Mind"—1968—#1 country—George Hamilton IV;
    1979—#1 country—Vern Gosdin
"I Wanna Live"—1968—top five pop—Glen Campbell
"It's My Time"—1969—top 20 country—Dolly Parton
"Indian Reservation"—1972—#1 pop—Mark Lindsay
    (Paul Revere & the Raiders)

In LaFayette, people had heard the hundreds of recordings
his songs had inspired, but few knew that the same illustrious
songwriter had come to live in their own town. They didn't
know that he was in fact an exile from his own super success.
None knew then about his story, the struggles that prompted
him to move away from his turbulent world in Music City. Had
they known, they would have been astounded by the unusual

legacy of a man almost drowned by his own accomplishments.

John D. Loudermilk came into the world in Durham, North Carolina. His mother, formerly a missionary to the Cherokee Indians in the Carolina mountains, along with John's father, part Cherokee, were members of the Salvation Army. Resultingly, John's musical and religious background were much influenced by that church. Singing on street corners, beating a bass drum, collecting food, participating in the active church youth group—all of his happy early years were closely involved with the Salvation Army.

As a tender-hearted ten-year-old boy, he started a lifelong relationship with Jesus Christ.

It was one night in church. During the invitation my mother noticed my nervousness and asked, "Are you convicted?"

I was, so I went down front to this trunk-shaped altar. With my mother and dad kneeling on either side, I gave my heart to God. There were people kneeling all around. It was such a moving, meaningful experience, and from that day on it's been real to me. Like a never-ending rubber-ball cycle, I've drifted away from Him and back to Him, but I've never left Him and I've never forgotten my salvation experience.

All of his musical roots started in that musically fertile organization. The founder of the movement, General William Booth, was credited with saying, "Why should the devil have all of the good music?" As a result, Salvation Army street and church meetings are always marked by spirited orchestrations. Not only did John D. learn to play many instruments, the trumpet, trombone, drums, guitar, harmonica, he also developed his strong singing voice.

Starting when he was eleven years old, John had a band and a radio show. When he was fourteen, his dad had a heat stroke, so John began booking his band outside of the church to help support the family. Finding himself torn between two sets of values, the dance halls and the church, John D. felt an intensely growing pull from both sides. That tension broke with an unusual circumstance.

One Sunday night, we were on a street corner holding an open-air meeting. The night before I had played for a dance in Durham. One of my high school buddies drove past the street meeting and yelled, "Hey, Loudermilk—let's go get drunk again like we did last night!"

It was just a joke, but there I was with my Salvation Army uniform on and the church members all around. It really threw me. I was trying to be a band musician and still be in our fundamental church.

Well, it got to me. Sensitive people always go off half-cocked anyway, taking things personal, but it threw me into an inner turmoil. I stopped going to church.

John D. Loudermilk continued to help support the family through his band work and artistic endeavors, doing showroom windows, etc., though he no longer took part in church work. As he reached the end of his high school, he began to turn to songwriting. His very first song was a less-than-illustrious triumph when he wrote the class song for his Durham High School graduating class—new words for "Anchors Away."

While continuing to dabble with his new songwriting hobby, John started working as the art director for television station WTVD, also doing a daily program for the Durham facility. It was at WTVD that the wheels of success started moving.

I was in my office downstairs getting ready for the show, when the song "Rose and a Baby Ruth" came to me. I don't know why I was selected to write the song, but it came so I wrote it. I ran upstairs and did it that day on the television show.

People started calling in—they liked it. Then Orville Campbell called—he was a record producer for George Hamilton IV. The next thing I knew we had a hit; I was a songwriter and George was a star.

With his first royalty check, he bought a house in Durham for his parents, then moved to Buies Creek, North

Carolina, to begin studying at Campbell College. *More than anything, I spent a year and a half trying to hear what kids were into musically.*

Continuing to write more songs, John got married and moved to Washington, D. C., where the newlyweds lived for a year. Finally, in 1958 John made an all-out assault on Nashville. There were no welcoming parties. There were no gigantic shock waves. The town seemed little impressed with his past pen-performances.

He gave himself one year to make it or break it in Nashville, but could find little more than some session work. The year-end deadline came swiftly with John no closer to initial success than when he came. Two days before the year was terminated, John started packing his clothing back at the small apartment.

I was doing some guitar back-up on a session that day with Chet Atkins. He invited me to lunch afterwards. I had been doing a lot of praying—"Lord, let me get some kind of a break."

Chet asked me, "John, how would you like to work for me?" I couldn't believe it; I was so happy. Chet didn't even know until later how close I came to leaving town.

The flight from obscurity to success was both swift and certain. John split the time during the next few years simultaneously working at three enviable jobs: with Chet in RCA's Artist and Repertory Department, with George Morgan and his television show, and with Jim Denny writing songs for Cedarwood Publishing Company. It was at Cedarwood that he met Marijohn Wilkin. Marijohn and John quickly put their talents together to write "Waterloo," a number one, million-selling hit for Stonewall Jackson. That was just the beginning.

From Cedarwood, John moved his writing efforts to Acuff-Rose Publishing Company. More than ever his songs began hitting, not just in America, but, even more so, in England. Number one discs flowed from Laudermilk's busy pen. It was an exciting period, for John and for Nashville's Music Row.

It was a beautiful time. Nashville had been fighting for recognition and was just starting to achieve it. Elvis was beginning to record there. Country music was becoming a giant industry. Nashville was really starting to happen.

It seemed to be a mind-boggling experience for an unknown young man from Durham to suddenly be caught in fame's flash flood. His own recordings were striking. Even religion became a social ladder-climb. Life was one big glittering flame.

I got "professional." All of a sudden I had huge sums of money, and even larger amounts of recognition were dropped on somebody who was not prepared for it all.

It's difficult to describe or define what happens to you. You get kind of a sneering attitude; an unreal syndrome like an insanity; a deviation from the norm. I guess it's like this for anyone swept up into New York or Hollywood or Nashville—it's a life based on unreality.

He churned out hit after hit through the sixties. Though many Nashville songwriters experienced a creative drouth during the Beatle/protest period, John always seemed to be happening, having song after song topping the country and pop charts.

However, beyond all the glistening awards and glowing achievements, John D. experienced the growing anguish of trying to fit the unreal surface world with his inner being. Once a man has feasted on the peace of God, he cannot live contentedly on the world's candy.

I got into the whole Nashville scene, but after fourteen years, the whole thing accumulated. I got divorced. My personal problems mounted. Finally I just had to get away.

He remarried and left with his two boys and new wife for a hiatus in England. The boys were enrolled in an English school for a term; then the whole family hired on to help take a 110-foot long sailing vessel from Northern Germany to the South of France.

The change in lifestyle had been a terrific experience for the whole family. Each of the boys reached manhood with the unlimited opportunity to develop individual talents. The oldest son is studying engineering in college. The middle eighteen-year-old is the fledging young artist, also in college. The youngest, who is still in high school, a musician, has already worked recording sessions on Chet Atkins "The Night Atlanta Burned" album. He also wrote "Sonora" which is on the recording. John and Suzie and their two youngest sons recently moved into a newly-built home in Baton Rouge. Life has never looked more beautiful to them. Even John's songs are experiencing revivals—for example, Vern Gosdin's "Break My Mind," a top ten chart hit in 1979.

It seems our reality has been established with the common people. Sometimes when I go back to Nashville to dub the demo tapes and do business there, I see so many people into the whole star-image thing. When you've been away, it baffles you to see it again—to imagine that you were once a part of it.

I remember one time a year or so after we left Nashville, my wife and I visited there again. After staying there for a few days, we got into the car to go back to Louisiana and went out on the highway. As we were leaving, I looked at Suzie, both of us with tears running, and I said, "I know now that we did the right thing."

It took a big step to leave the creative forces there. It had taken fourteen years of climbing up the social and music industry's ladder. He was on the CMA and NARAS boards, which John says "made me a double phony—business and creative people are on two different levels."

So he left Nashville to get a grip on the valued things: God, his talent, his family. God made it all beautiful once more. Today he courts and romances the idea of someday returning to live in Nashville. Thanks to God, the next time it will be different.

W. ELMO MERCER—NASHVILLE'S BEST KNOWN, UNKNOWN SONGWRITER
Arranger and writer of top Gospel songs, "Each Step I Take," "The Time Is Now"

Without pretense or pageantry, this former Louisiana bank teller continues to be one of the most dominating forces in Gospel music. Not only does he write legendary songs ("Each Step I Take," "The Way That He Loves," "Lonely Road Up Calvary's Way"—songs recorded by virtually every gospel artist and many "name" secular singers), but perhaps his most notable accomplishments are least known.

He was born in Grant Parish, Louisiana, on a cold February morning—1932. His parents were "every-time-the-doors-are-open" Baptists, so it is no surprise that Elmo was "born again" nine years later.

I was brought up in church, the First Baptist, in Winnfield,

Louisiana. I was taught to read the Bible daily and study my Sunday school lesson. That reading really was what turned me to the Lord. I was reading my Sunday school lesson one Friday—something I read made me realize that I needed to accept the Lord as my OWN personal Saviour. Something touched me to help me see myself as I was.

On Saturday I went to talk with my pastor, Rev. H.H. McBride, who led me to the Lord. The next day when the invitation was given at the end of the sermon, I went down front and made a public profession.

That was June, 1941. In November, he was baptized and became a member of that church.

He graduated with excellent grades from high school, and soon began working as a bank teller in his native Winnfield, Louisiana. He married the former Marcia Fletcher in 1954. *Marcia was four and a half years younger than I was, so I never paid a lot of attention to her when I used to pal around with her sister who was the same age as myself. When she reached her last year in high school, I suddenly realized that the little girl had grown up!*

Characteristically, Elmo recalls the details. Details are important to him.

Our first date was on the eight of January—(which also, by the way, is the anniversary of the Battle of New Orleans!). Two and a half months later, I gave her a diamond ring—reminds me of the Ralph Carmichal song, "I found What I Wanted!"

We were married in October; spent $55 on a three-day honeymoon in Hot Springs, Arkansas!

Thus far, his story sounds typical enough to be a carbon copy for numerous other men who live in any other town in any other state of the country; however, while the surface seemed commonplace, an unusual talent began to unfold on a national scale.

At the age of fourteen, Elmo wrote his first song, "A Glimpse of Jesus." For five years he continued to write, and at age nineteen submitted several songs to the John T. Benson Publishing Company in Nashville; unbelievably, this prestigious company bought this young teenager's first works.

That began a lifelong relationship and friendship between Elmo and the Bensons. The songwriting was "just" a hobby for young Mercer who finished high school with plans to spend the rest of his life as a bank teller. More songs that he wrote were published, but perhaps his best-known composition was written as a nineteen-year-old, "Each Step I Take." This song was recorded first by country giant, Slim Whitman, on Columbia Records, later by radio and television personality Ray Robles on the Christian Faith label.

But despite the increasing success—in characteristic fashion—Elmo had no long-range, flamboyant plans.

I worked as a bank teller for nine years, starting soon after I finished high school. I still love banking, and appreciated being in the banking business. My wife worked at the Louisiana State Welfare Department. Songwriting was just "on the side."

I was excited to be able to get some of my songs published. You can imagine how excited I was at nineteen, getting my first songs accepted; then later as more were accepted and recorded, but I never considered being anything other than a bank teller.

My wife and I would come up to Nashville every so often. Mr. Benson would settle up with me and decide what new songs he wanted. That's the way it continued for several years.

A new avenue opened for Elmo when, during a visit, Mr. Benson asked Mercer to listen to a recording. "Side one, song two," Benson said, "take it down and arrange it."

It took me four days to do that one song with the four parts on paper!

That one song—four days assignment seems almost humorous for the man who now arranges much more detailed songs, sometimes as many as six or seven a day.

Still, despite the sold-songs and growing experience, no major changes were planned. The Louisiana lifestyle was comfortable and secure.

I had paid holidays, a bonus, and vacation at the bank, so I thought that I had a good thing going. I didn't really feel that I was well-grounded in music since I had only taken piano two years during the fourth and fifth grades. My wife taught me how to read and write shaped notes.

So with little formal music training, Mercer continued to work at the bank in Louisiana, and write . . . and write . . . and write. To date he has written over 1,000 songs with about 400 published and/or copyrighted and/or recorded—a mind-staggering success in an industry that stands in awe of a writer of few recorded songs. Yet, this unbelievable catalog is just the beginning of the talents to this incredible man.

After much cajoling, he moved to Nashville to work for the growing John T. Benson Publishing Company as a music editor. That was 1961; he was only the sixth employee for the now gargantuan organization. For a year he worked without a piano in a little cubbyhole, arranging music in his head, then taking the penciled paper home to try it on his piano. Outside arranging for other artists and writers helped supplement his small income. He did all the sheet music arranging for the Benson Company until recently—a fact that means little to most until they consider that for each of these thousands of songs, Elmo took the basic idea from a lead sheet or recording given to him by the "writer," and worked it into a full composition.

The many writers who have used his talent include Dallas Holm, Lanny Wolfe, Henry Slaughter, Dottie Rambo, Jimmie Davis, Gordon Jensen, and perhaps the greatest—Bill and Gloria Gaither.

Case in point:

Doug Oldham introduced "The King Is Coming" when we were at the Christian Booksellers Convention in Minneapolis.

At that time I was getting $20 a song for arranging. Bill Gaither was excited at the tremendous response at the noon luncheon when the song was first sung, so he gave me a lead sheet of it. I worked until two A.M. without a piano in that Minneapolis Hotel room, arranging it in my head then putting it on paper. The next morning I ran into Mosie Lister, bought an eight-cent stamp from him, and dropped it in the mail to the typesetter.

The rest is history, and it has been repeated over and over with little public notice directed toward the man who is the powerful force behind the scene of so many of today's writers.

Playing "second fiddle" to so many great writers would cause most people to react with envy, but not Elmo Mercer. Somehow for this gentle man, this humility is sort of expected.

It doesn't bother me. I just love being a part. I often think, "Here I am, arranging for a great company and writing songs. What a life!"

I brown-bag my lunch to work so I don't have to kill an hour going out to lunch. I enjoy "slaving over a hot piano!"

With an almost childish delight, he shares an arrangement he has just completed, playing a special section of sixteenth notes along with a Henry Slaughter recording. He sings and plays proficiently, yet has no ambition to tour as an instrumentalist or singer.

I never wanted to be a professional performer. It doesn't scare me, but I just don't care for it. I'm doing some personal appearances now, doing some choral work in churches sometimes, but I don't want to be a professional performer.

I'm just an old "country boy" with only two years training. I've always felt inferior musically to people like Ronn Huff and Rick Powell—people like that with all their degrees and abilities. I reckon my thirty-one years of experience help "bridge the gap" somewhat!

Despite his misgivings, Elmo continues to blaze a musical trail that is so incredible that it has become almost commonplace. He recently had a song, "The Time Is Now," selected for inclusion in Broadman's *Baptist Hymnal*—the hymnbook for millions of Southern Baptists. He arranged and compiled the souvenier songbook for a recent Christian Booksellers Convention in Kansas City. Two of his songs were sung at the last Southern Baptist Convention in Kansas City. He just completed arranging and editing the 545 songs included in the *New National Baptist Hymnal*, songbook for America's largest Black Baptist denomination. In addition to continuing to write classic gospel songs that artists continue to record with much success, he was recently notified of his tenth award from the Standard Awards Panel of the American Society of Composers, Authors, and Publishers, of which he has been a member more than 20 years.

Yet, he is hardly a larger-than-life personality. Hardly. He is a refreshing person, genuine and loving. He is steady and dependable. Since thirteen years of age, for over thirty-two years, Elmo has been a church-elected musician, serving presently as the pianist at Park Avenue Baptist Church in Nashville.

Typically, instead of ego-building and gilt-edged name-throwing conversation, Elmo would much rather talk about simpler things—the song he's working on; the river boats and barges plowing through the Cumberland River behind the gigantic Benson Company complex; and a life-long dream that he has finally realized—a 70-acre farm of his own some 60 miles from Nashville.

We raise Angus cattle and horses. We have a tractor, wagon, implements, garden—the whole bit. As a kid, I lived next to Charley Taylor's Horse Farm—so I always had this dream to have a farm.

He lives in an unspectacular but tasteful home on a 50-acre tract, twelve miles west of Nashville with his lovely wife, Marcia. His son, Elmo Jr. (Bill), is a junior student at Middle Tennessee State majoring in Aerospace Technology.

Daughter, Kellye Dianne, is a sophomore high school student.

There are many stories about successful people, dramatic, stunning, shocking, unbelievable stories. Then there are just-as-miraculous epochs that are more common and typical. Elmo Mercer remains something of an uncanny mixture untouched by success. No pretense; no pageantry—just commonly incredible.

BILLY ROY MOORE—SHEPHERD OF MANY NASHVILLE STARS

**Pastor of The Lord's Chapel—fellowship includes
Connie Smith Haynes, Barbara Mandrell,
Barbara Fairchild, Archie Jordan**

Photo: Phil Egert

Billy Roy Moore and Connie Smith with PTL Club's Tammy Bakker
and Henry Harrison.

Few men are able to lead others by true example. Most leaders must push, cojole, or browbeat. Especially is this true in churches. Billy Roy Moore is a unique follow-the-leader shepherd. It shows up in many gentle ways—through the testimonies of many stars who attend his church as they speak of "his Christlikeness," through the rapid and successful development of Nashville's Lord's Chapel, and mostly through watching and listening to Billy Moore.

In some ways his life and background is not cluttered with pseudo-dramatic stories (on the surface at least). In an era that makes instant heroes of new Christians who have tragic/triumphant sagas, the simplicity of Billy's life actually highlights the messages he shares today.

Billy was reared in a Christian home in North Little Rock, Arkansas. When he was only eight he accepted Jesus Christ as his personal Saviour.

My mother was always singing "My Jesus, My Jesus." This made an impression—that He was that important to her. Anyway I was sitting beside her during a church service (the First Assembly of God), and as I was thinking about the song, I asked her, "Can He be my Jesus, too?" She prayed with me. As soon as I accepted the Lord I also knew that I would be a preacher.

From that time I dreamed about being a preacher. All my friends and family knew I was gonna be a pentecostal preacher!

I never went through the rebellious stage. I mean I wasn't right with the Lord all the time, but all life as a family was centered around Jesus. My parents were very encouraging in this. In fact, the two worst punishments in our family was not to be able to eat and not to get to go to church.

This environment of absolute belief in God's prominence and power was to form the basis for Billy Moore's life. Even as a child he was taught (often first-hand) to believe in miracles through prayer. Crippling accidents when he was four, five, and sixteen were overcome supernaturally by the family's prayers, especially the near-tragedy when he was a teenager.

I was on my paper route, 3:00 A.M. Sunday morning, and as I rode my bicycle I was hit by a '39 Pontiac. When they got me to the hospital, they found my left arm was jaggedly broken and my left hand was cut badly. My folks were notified. They began praying on the way to the hospital. Before they arrived, the doctors had left the room momentarily before coming back to set the bone and sew the wounds. When the doctors came back in I said, "The Lord just healed me!" It was true, the doctors knew it was miraculous. They had just diagnosed it before and now—just minutes later—the bone was mended and the cuts were gone!

*They released me even before my parents arrived and I
threw my paper route that morning.*

With this day-by-day faith-heritage, it is not surprising
that Billy was preaching by the time he reached eighteen.
Soon afterwards he began formally studying for the ministry
at South Central Bible College, Hot Springs, Arkansas. There
—most importantly—he met and married Pixie Berkihiser in
1950. One year later, after graduation, the couple began
traveling as evangelists, but their ministry was almost terminated before it had barely begun.

*It was in December, 1951. We were heading toward
Eldorado, Arkansas, in our '39 Packard Coupe. Pixie was
asleep and I noticed her car door was not completely closed. I
reached over to pull it closed, and as I did I hit a soggy road
shoulder. We careened out of control across a bridge abut-
ment. It slung me out of the car. I saw the top of the car about
to roll over me. I remember only praying that God would take
care of my baby (Pixie). She was instantly knocked out and
never knew what happened until she woke up sometime later.
Other than bruises and being shaken, she was okay, but I had
a broken pubic and pelvic bone. I also had internal injuries
and my nervous system was shot. The doctors told my family
that even if I lived, I'd be flat on my back for six weeks and
crippled the rest of my life.*

*However, in ten days I was out of the hospital. In ten more
days I was propped up with crutches and preaching. The
following Tuesday after that, I was completely healed and
playing football. Everyday I still run for Jesus. I'm fifty now
and still playing tackle football.*

God still works miracles. This same God has had an obvious hand on Billy Moore through a steadily progressive life
ministry. After traveling the evangelism circuit, Billy and
Pixie (and their six-month-old son, Charles Merlin—their only
child who is now a young Nashville songwriter) moved to
Nashville in 1953 where he served as assistant pastor of First
Assembly of God. From there the family pioneered four

churches in Tennessee—Millington (eighteen months in service), Clarksville (eighteen months—he worked three different jobs, averaging 2½ hours sleep each night), Soddy-Daisy (eleven years), and East Nashville (four years.).

Then in August, 1971, the Moores began—through a 23rd Psalm House Ministry—to build the Lord's Chapel, from an initial six hardy souls to a present 1,200. During the years since the inception over 3,000 young people have found the Lord and been trained for His service through Billy Moore's ministry. One secret to the solid success is the thirty-five weekly home Bible study groups and an overall foundation upon God's Word.

We emphasize the Word and worship. It's certainly not a one-man show. In fact, we do some things very differently, we give an altar call before I preach. Those wanting to be saved, healed, or to receive their prayer language are asked to go upstairs where the sixteen elders and twenty counsellors minister to them.

We feel it's important to have a body ministry. I guess I'm more of a sheep dog than anything—a helping ministry. When I preach, we go through the Bible—a chapter at a time. I emphasize for the people to not accept it just because I say it. I've found that if I share the Word, people get hungry to feed on it even more on their own.

I'm amazed at the way God reveals things even while I teach. It's wonderful to see the Holy Spirit move as He confirms the Word. We don't preach miracles as such—we preach Jesus, but it's amazing to see the miracles happen.

I've learned in all my ministry that I'm not to preach my frustrations or anxieties. I teach Jesus—then He can conform us to His image. It's His battle anyway. It's not my congregation—it's His. I'm just a vessel standing up sharing His Word. The vessel isn't important—the treasure is.

And about the constant stream of celebrities who visit the Lord's Chapel out of peace-seeking curiosity?

I really do nothing special. They (the stars) want you to

treat them as just everyday people. Jesus is the answer to all their problems so I minister personally to them just like anyone else. If I would try to just please them it would be unfair to everyone. I find that everyone is comfortable with this type of ministry.

In a ministry as much in the public eye as his, Billy has seen difficult times, of course, including two destroying fires (one accidental, one from a thrown Molotov cocktail). And there are the occasional telephone threats from Satan worshippers in the Nashville area.

I've found that it's best to answer them by saying, "You can't do anything to us because you operate on fear and God has not given us the spirit of fear. In fact, if you are not careful, you will be delivered from Satan yourself!" We've had people delivered from Satan worship through this witness.

Not only is the church reaching the unusual, illustrious, and everyday, the Lord's Chapel is reaching out with far-flung future plans: a 105-acre tract (purchased at one-fourth the market cost), a new auditorium, school, nursing home, and possibly a children's home. The pastor's eyes sparkle with determined excitement as he discusses the plans. There is little doubt that God will continue the unusual blessings. To Billy Roy Moore, miraculous is normal, which incidently, is the way Jesus planned it to be as He spoke to His followers 2,000 years ago:

> "In solemn truth I tell you, anyone believing in me shall do the same miracles I have done, and even greater ones, because I am going to be with the Father. You can ask him for *anything*, using my name, and I will do it, for this will bring praise to the Father because of what I, the Son, will do for you. Yes, ask *anything*, using my name, and I will do it!" (John 14:12-14 LB).

RON PETERSON—TOMORROW'S GONNA BE BETTER

**Band member—"Ronny and the Daytonas"; songwriter—
"Sitting in Atlanta Station," "Nighthawk"; and past president—
Nashville Songwriters Association International**

Ron Peterson with Maggie Cavendar (executive secretary of the
Nashville Songwriters Association International).

Since 1929, Peterson Machinery Company has been a successful business. John Christian Peterson came from Sweden
to start the fledgling venture. Today, his grandson, Ron
Peterson, manages the Nashville base for a constantly growing industrial supplier that has four stores in Tennessee, selling construction equipment throughout the Southeastern
United States.

Though the position he now holds would be an outstanding
achievement for anyone, that shirt-and-tie status is but one
side of this artistic "Jekyll and Hyde" story. In addition, Ron
Peterson is a successful songwriter, has performed with a top
pop group, is the past president of the Nashville Songwriters

Association International, has been a leading race car driver, and, most importantly, is a born-again Christian.

It was not always so. The past is as unusual as the present.

He was raised in east Nashville, the blonde-kid-next-door with a background deep-rooted in the active music program at Grace Baptist Church. He sang in a church choir from the time he was six years old. His mother was a featured soloist in the church.

Ron's spiritual life was initiated at that church by the pastor, Dr. Stigler.

I was saved when I was twelve years old on a Sunday night. I remember it vividly. The invitation was given; I wanted to go forward and was afraid. There was another young boy beside me the same age as myself, and probably if he hadn't gone up I wouldn't have. He had enough "guts" to take that first step and I followed, praying and accepting the Lord as my Saviour.

Though he was a product of a broken marriage, and though he was anything but a young saint, he still managed to forego many traumas that trouble countless teens. Life was wrapped around school, church, and music.

It gave me a very stable adolescence. I didn't have the growing pains so many kids do. I guess one reason was my close relationship with my parents and the Lord.

He attended Madison High School (a Nashville suburb) for two years and went into the senior year at Castle Heights Military School in Lebanon, Tennessee, skipping a year because of high grades. Though he had junior high school dreams of playing football and being a doctor (quite a combination), his ninety-four pound freshman frame forced Ron to find other pursuits besides playing with the laced pigskin. He trained for the tennis, wrestling, and baseball teams, and turned his attention to music (vocal, french horn, and trumpet).

Graduating from high school in 1963, Ron enrolled as a freshman at the University of Tennessee in Knoxville.

It was one of the best places in the world to stop being a Christian. That was the wildest year of my life.

I had never really been away from home that much, and suddenly I ran headlong into so many different kinds of people. I guess everyone goes through a similiar period at sometime in his life. I stopped going to church. It was a testing era as I tried to sort out my thoughts and beliefs.

The drinking and wild parties happened often. Though still technically a student, he turned from academic pursuits to a new musical endeavor, a folk group aptly named, "The Wayward Three." With Ron playing rhythm guitar, the group became a favorite at numerous parties in the Knoxville area.

Coming back from school for the 1964 summer vacation, Ron was asked by a neighbor friend, Lynn Williams, if he would like to join a touring group.

Lynn was in Bucky Wilkin's group (Ronny and the Daytonas), and they had a big hit going all over the nation. "GTO" was breaking all over the place, eventually selling over a million copies, rated number one in many places.

Promoters were planning on booking Ronny and the Daytonas all over the world, including a Christmas USO trip to Japan and Okinawa. Bobby Russell, Bergen White, Buzz Cason, and Lynn were the band members.

Of course, when they asked me to go, I was at the age when I would do anything—"Sure, let's go!"—so I went to rehearsal, met Bucky and the group, and signed on. Bucky was terrific on the guitar; he showed me how to play the chords and surfing-type licks. It was the first time I had played an electric guitar, but I jumped in and did it anyway.

With no intention of going back to school, especially with some "green stuff" flashed in front of them, the group plunged into the concert tours with "GTO," "Sandy," and "Bucket T" striking all over. After the first weeks of constant concerts, the young men were seasoned professionals, playing to gigantic screaming throngs of kids.

We didn't know it at the time, but we were at the very top of pop showbiz. It was the big time, though to us it was just a big game.

We played with groups like the Animals, Beach Boys, and Shangra-Las. We toured with Dick Clark's "Caravan of Stars," appeared on "American Bandstand," as well as the USO tour.

By the time Ron reached his nineteenth birthday, he had experienced more fame than most people know in a lifetime. The months of nonstop traveling started losing some of the glitter.

In 1966, Ron left the group. He got married shortly afterwards, though the marriage seemed doomed from the beginning for the diametrically-opposed couple. *It wasn't just difficult trying to blend our lifestyles, it was impossible. A year after we were married, it ended in divorce.*

The whirlwind years had taken their toll, especially for Ron's spiritual side.

I had very little religious life. I wasn't going to church. I was changing some of my values. I don't think that I was ever doubtful of my own Christianity; I had just gotten out of any personal relationship with the Lord.

Though the traveling and subsequent marriage faded away, a new pastime began.

I had known Marijohn Wilkin from the Daytonas' days since she was Bucky's mother, but about 1967 I started hanging around her house more and more. It was the most creative place in the world—really! All kinds of songwriters and pickers would sit around song-swapping. Kris Kristofferson, Chris Gantry, Mel Tillis—so many big writers.

If you didn't have some new songs you had written, you just didn't have anything to say. The only reason that I started writing songs was so I could enter into the conversation and jam sessions.

Being in such close association with such heavyweight talents helped the young writer develop his cradle-stage creative craft.

Having access to their talented minds was a once-in-a-lifetime experience. Kris was always truthful in critiquing your new material. We weren't that close, but he kinda regarded me more like a little brother than anything.

Marijohn was the greatest song-doctor in the world, though I never knew her to claim credit for helping any of the writers who came to her house. She could move a verse or add an extra chorus or bridge to make a plain song into a great hit song.

Although he was working as the national sales manager for Royal American Records and promotion manager for Buddha Records, songwriting became an increasingly satisfying hobby, especially with Ron's first big song being recorded in 1968—Nat Stucky's "Sitting In Atlanta Station" (co-written with Van Trevor) that hit the top ten national charts, also winning an ASCAP award.

I had some songs recorded before, but I'll never forget that ego-boosting experience of having that first big hit with one of your songs. I went over to Marijohn's house not long after it started getting a lot of airplay, really happy about it all.

She said, "Wait 'till they send you your check. They pay you for having this kind of fun!" I remember saying back to her that I hoped it never stopped being this exciting or fun.

Boosted by the initial success, Ron decided in 1971 to go into full-time songwriting on a four-hundred-dollar-a-month draw from Atlanta Music. By that time, he had remarried. He and Kathie moved to backwoods America, Mulberry, Tennessee.

I spent a whole year writing songs and starving to death. It taught me a lot. I had to get down and write a lot of songs at some point to develop my craftsmanship. A lot of people write that first big song, then never do any more.

Having that first song recorded is a successful step, but the truly successful songwriter will continue climbing, regardless of the results.

I was learning that having success early can really be quite damaging—you start right off thinking that you already know it all. Then when the next song doesn't hit, you find out that you really don't know much at all.

Not only was that year-long retreat in rural Tennessee an opportunity to develop musically, it was also an invaluable short course in human relations and faith-in-action.

I did a real personal turnaround. It wasn't a very visible thing, but my ability to accept people like they are was largely attributable to my wife.

We lived in this big old house in a small town, an entirely different life for me since I had never met people like this in school or traveling or writing. I learned how to work for the first time in my life. I helped on the farms: killing hogs, stripping tobacco, working in the fields. I never got money for it but the experience taught me to like work, and the value of hard work.

These were real grass-roots Christians. It was about this time that I started getting back to my religious beliefs. I got to witness a lot of faith there in Mulberry. Many of them were so poor and had very little, yet they were the happiest people in the world. Their Christianity was real.

Armed with a renewed personal faith in Christ and a new vigor for life, Ron returned after the year to get down to work, for his family's company, for the Lord, and with his songwriting talents.

In 1975, Ron wrote "Touch The Hand" that Conway Twitty recorded. "Touch The Hand" skyrocketed to the legendary number one position on national charts, selling 700,000 copies.

Besides having other songs recorded, Ron released several songs under his stage name, John Deer. Several hit airplay charts, the largest being the "Battle Hymn of Lt. Calley."

Currently, more songs from Ron's busy pen are echoing throughout Nashville's recording studios and the nation's radio stations. "Nighthawk," one of Ron's latest, was recently recorded by C.W. McCall. But writing is just one avenue of expression for the all-American success story. He is a highly respected businessman, music industry spokesman, songwriter, publisher (he and Marijohn Wilkin own Meredith Music). Yet there is more.

Spiritually, I'm closer to the Lord than ever before. I realize that my relationship has got to be a personal thing to be satisfying.

I'm just now reaping a lot of benefits out of my faith that I couldn't even see earlier. The peace that goes with a personal belief in Christ is worth everything. I'm able to talk about my faith without being ashamed of it anymore. No longer is God some mysterious Being, He is a personal Lord.

At home, Ron and his lovely wife Kathie have three children whom he instantly labels "great kids"—Keith, Ron Jr., and Meredith.

Tomorrow's going to be better for this businessman songwriter, especially if his life follows past performances. It's been a steady succession of "gettin' better." There have been numerous valleys mixed in with the mountaintops, but with God at the controls, life has to get better. For the dedicated Christian, this life is just a little hors d'oeuvre of the feast to come.

> "Let that therefore abide in you, which ye have heard from the beginning. If that which ye have heard from the beginning shall remain in you, ye also shall continue in the Son, and in the Father.
>
> And this is the promise that He hath promised us, even eternal life" (1 John 2:24-25).

JIMMY SNOW—GOD NEVER PROMISED
IT WOULD BE EASY
Hank Snow's famous son; pastor of many Music City personalities

Jimmy Snow is one of God's interesting paradoxes. He is the son of Hank Snow, one of country's top singers for three decades; however, with all the opportunities given to join his father at the top, he rebelled as a teenager—popping pills, drinking—literally "raising hell." When Jimmy's professional career did explode—record hits, national television appearances, friendships with numerous greats, including Elvis Presley; then, Jimmy turned his back on his rising stardom. At the height of a flourishing career he became a Christian, giving away a seemingly certain success.

Since then, as he has served the Lord through preaching, he has been both hated and loved by Nashville. As a minister, he has been instrumental in winning many well-known per-

sonalities and has been pastor to a mélange of artists—
Johnny Cash, Connie Smith, Eddie Miller, Billy Walker,
Jeannie C. Riley, Barbara Fairchild, Larry Gatlin; yet as his
Evangel Temple reached an all-time peak, Jimmy Snow's personal and professional life was split apart by a media-
splashed divorce. Though the rift mushroomed, seeming to
destroy Jimmy's entire ministry, then God began to have
the biggest, hard-fought victories.

Continually the paradoxes have mounted, yet the man
behind the unusual story is anything but confusing. He
comes on arrow-straight. There is no mistaking his motives
or actions.

He has made mistakes, which he willingly admits. But God
makes no mistakes, and when He created Jimmy Snow, He
knew the masterplan. He knew before hand the triumphs and
tragedies that His servant would go through. Little did Jimmy know the extent of paradox God's design would allow him
to experience. It's a good thing He didn't.

Life began for little Jimmie Rodgers Snow in Halifax, Nova
Scotia, born to Hank and Minnie Snow—poor parents from
farm backgrounds. Even before Jimmy (he changed the spell-
ing later) came into the world, his father lived and breathed
country music, in real life experiencing the hard times that he
would later popularize in classic recordings. The year the
baby was born, Hank cut his first record for RCA Victor.

From early childhood, Jimmy was primed to share the
stage with his famous "Singing Ranger" father. The family
toured the continent, eventually moving to Nashville when
the elder Snow joined the Grand Ole Opry. During concerts,
Jimmy was the small center of attention in the cute cowboy
suit who always stole the show from his popular, pleased dad.

A formal education was a practical impossibility for the
wandering minstrels. When Jimmy was in the classroom, he
created havoc—gambling, fighting, dipping girls' pigtails in
ink wells—generally causing gray hairs and headaches for
numerous teachers.

Already stealing money from his classmates and parents, Jimmy reached his sixteenth birthday with a vow never to return to school. Feeling "different" because of his background, the only thing he was happy at was appearing on the Opry alongside all the great performers: Roy Acuff, Ernest Tubb, Minnie Pearl, Red Foley, Hank Williams, and of course, his own top-rated father. A wild lifestyle became commonplace for the young singer despite the tragedy of several performer-friends.

Stories about Red Foley, Hank Williams, and others around the Opry didn't sway me. As a young teenager, I couldn't see myself ending up this way. I told myself, "It'll never happen to me."

Unfortunately, it did happen. He became a chronic and acknowledged "pillhead" and alcoholic. Numerous attempts by his father and mother to stop the destructive force failed. As Jimmy's appetite for liquor and partying grew, so did his professional popularity, this time more as Jimmy Snow rather than "Hank Snow's son."

In 1954, Hank Snow and Colonel Tom Parker joined forces to begin Jamboree Attractions. Jimmy was signed to perform on tours with Mother Maybelle and the Carter Sisters, the Duke of Paducah, Faron Young, Marty Robbins, Andy Griffith, and a new unknown kid:

Elvis Presley joined our 1954 tour in Carlsbad, New Mexico. His name appeared 'way down the showbill, even below mine.

"Elvis the Pelvis," as he was already being called, sauntered onstage in black pants with pink stripes down the legs, black jacket, and pink shirt with the collar turned up. He drove the females into hysterics.

As we moved from city to city, the crowds got bigger and noisier. It was wild, crazy, weird, scary.

Elvis and I made a strange pair. I wore a straight cowboy suit and sat around trying to think of something to say. He didn't smoke, drink, or curse, and sirred and ma'amed everybody over twenty-one. On the other hand, I had all the

111

vices and wore a chip on my shoulder. But we both liked girls for sex and boys for company.

Even during the early tours, the musicians seemed to have an endless supply of pills and liquor. Alcohol and drugs began to dim both the ambition and career of Jimmy Snow. As 1955 passed, Jimmy became more and more of an embarrassment to his famous father. Finally, deciding to do everyone a favor by getting away from Nashville and showbusiness, young Snow enlisted in the Air Force.

January 3, 1956, two days before leaving for boot camp, tragedy struck. His '54 Oldsmobile was hit head-on by a drunken driver. The one-hundred and five mile-an-hour blurr exploded into the front of Jimmy's auto. Jimmy's broken, almost lifeless body was rushed to the emergency room.

Somehow, he lived. Sackfuls of mail poured into the hospital room. Thirty-eight days later he was released on crutches to go home.

If Dad was hoping the wreck would turn me around, he was hoping in vain. I was only grudgingly grateful for their care, and only a little thankful to be alive. I still couldn't see much worth living for, except partying and womanizing.

Perhaps because of the wreck-publicity, or for some unknown reason, Jimmy started experiencing a new popularity upsurge. Suddenly the breaks came. Show dates and record sales increased. He signed a RCA Victor recording contract, and began guesting on the Opry.

Everything began to click. He was one of the first country artists to be showcased in Hollywood, appearing on several television shows, the Lawrence Welk Show alone had an estimated 70 million viewers.

Back in Nashville, he was making plans to marry Carol Lee Cooper (daughter of Opry greats—Wilma Lee and Stoney Cooper), but still couldn't shake the old liquor and drug habits.

Then on November 27, 1957, the end *and* the beginning came. In his bedroom, he was torn apart by dreams of fame confronted with the Holy Spirit's conviction for his past. Fighting the mixed emotions, Jimmy suddenly decided that suicide seemed to be the only way out.

I reached for the snub-nosed Smith and Wesson revolver I always carried. This wasn't the first time I had contemplated suicide. A few weeks before I had swallowed a handful of barbiturates only to awaken to the realization that I had failed in yet another endeavor. Then I tried driving my car into a telephone pole at a high speed but didn't have the guts.

The gun seemed to make my fingers itch, as if it were daring me to use it. I stuck the barrel in my mouth, determined to show myself that I could pull the trigger. I still couldn't do it. I didn't have the nerve.

I threw the gun on the bed and wobbled toward the door. I had to get away. Away from myself. Away from my sin.

I stepped into the bitter cold night barefoot and shirtless. The frigid air came as a shock to my lungs, but did little to clear my foggy brain. I started running. Running blindly into the darkness. Somehow I got to the mail box (at the end of the driveway in front of Hank Snow's house) and there I fell on my face on the cold ground and began crying out to God.

"God, I'm miserable. God, I'm hopeless. God, I'm no good. God, nobody can help me. You've got to help me. God, if You're really there, help me. Please, God. Please. I'm sorry. Oh, God, forgive me."

The words came rushing out in a torrent. Louder and louder. Porch lights came on across the street. The neighbors must have figured I was coming home from another drunk.

"Please, God, hear me. Forgive me. Jesus, help me. Save me. Oh, please. Please."

I must have prayed an hour in the freezing cold. I would have stayed there all night, I was so desperate. But sometime, somehow, I reached out in faith and complete dependence on God. All I know is that my mind cleared and I was filled with an overflowing peace. I knew my past had been forgiven. That my future belonged to Him. God had not only accepted me; He was going to use me in His service.

That night was the end of an old life filled with so many particles that Jimmy was all too eager to forget. That night was even more so the beginning of a new life that would literally touch thousands. Prayer settled so many things.

Then next morning my mind was still whirling, but I was positive of two things—God had given me a new life and He had called me to preach. There could be no denying what had happened. I'd never be the same. I could not go back.

At twenty-two and sixteen respectively, Jimmy and Carol Lee began their life together soon after Jimmy's decision. The newlyweds and new Christians, traveling together with a touring Jamboree, reached a hard-fought decision to go into full-time evangelism.

The call to preach seemed absurd since before his salvation Jimmy had to get his stage courage from a bottle, but the baptism of the Holy Spirit changed all that. The change from cringing introvert to preaching extrovert was the beginning, but there were many problems in the future that almost swamped the young evangelist—crooked associates, financial pressure, criticism, lack of formal training, utter discouragement, shady financial dealings by some churches, and a general mistrust for this former showbiz singer by the church community. Somehow he survived, believing that "whatsoever God has started, He would finish." The difficult/invaluable on-the-job training prepared for bigger tests in the future.

In all of his preaching ministry, then or now, the main thrust has been soul-winning.

I always felt the biggest miracle was salvation. I saw drunks turn sober, unfaithful start loving their wives, kids get delivered from drugs, and many other types of transformations, all through the new birth and the power of the Spirit.

Especially in the Nashville area, many of the show business people came to hear the fiery young evangelist. As more and more of the greats found lasting peace through Jesus

114

Christ—T. Texas Tyler, Patsy Cline, and others—Jimmy began seeing the need for a permanent work among the music industry people in Nashville.

In addition, Carol Lee and Jimmy were starting to seek a place to put down secure home-ties, especially with the birth of their first child, Vanessa, on September 19, 1962. By 1965, the dream was realized; they came home to begin the Evangel Temple.

Stars of the singing trade supported the work and began attending. By 1968, the church was a well-known institution in music city.

Nowhere in Nashville, except at the Opry, could you find such a variety of country musicians. Choir and congregations were sprinkled with bits and pieces of professional bands and singers from just about every group on the Opry.

Also in 1968, the top-rated "Gospel Country" television broadcast started, featuring big name artists. Often the guest artists were reached by the very songs that they performed. Connie Smith, for example, wept through her rendition of "In The Garden," then was led to the Lord after the broadcast.

By 1972, the Evangel Temple was growing like wildfire, being named the fastest growing church in the entire Assemblies of God denomination. Numerous stars and townspeople found the Lord and became shoulder-to-shoulder members. Because of his own background, Jimmy Snow has a special insight and empathy for the needs of the lost.

Things never looked brighter or better as Jimmy left in October, 1972, to help Johnny Cash with the feature-length film "Gospel Road" to be done on location in Israel. The rosy appearance couldn't have been farther from the truth.

Returning to Nashville in November, his entire world split. Jimmy and Carol Lee's marriage ended in a divorce. There were many reasons. Each had developed his/her own world. Both had feet of clay. Satan had attacked head-on, with crushing heavy blows on both lives.

Newspapers and national pulp-periodicals mocked. Friends turned away. People left the church. Accusations flew. Ugly gossip spread.

Only because of God's healing power did either Carol Lee or Jimmy Snow survive. With the divorce finalized, Jimmy planned on resigning as pastor of Evangel Temple. Self-pity set in. Trying to put God first, ahead of his own family, had blown up in his face for all the world to see.

"Why?" The question was hurled. An answer came back from an ever-loving, ever-gentle Jesus Christ.

So that I might get the glory. You were riding high. You were the big wheel. The preacher everybody was bragging about. The one numbered among the celebrities.

Now I'm getting the glory. People are looking to Me, not Jimmy Snow. They're coming to Evangel Temple because of Me.

Somehow, at that point of almost quitting, the Lord began to sift the situation to suit Himself, etching miracle after miracle on a tragic, impossible plight.

Turning their back to the scars, the pastor and church started again. By late 1972, the church forged together enough to start the "Grand Ole Gospel" each Friday night at the Opry, and broadcasting services over WSM's 50,000-Watt Opry station.

In successive years the church has grown to a four to five-hundred member plateau, the newest effort being a magazine—*Grand Ole Gospel Time*. There are plans to begin a new television program.

Jimmy faced new problems when he remarried in 1975. The new bride, Dottie, was from a similar showbiz background. Her personal faith in the Lord, and her newborn love helped erase many problems. Somehow, despite arched eyebrow and frowns, the jigsaw puzzle started fitting together again.

Today, Jimmy Snow faces each day's tasks with more insight and intensity than many people realize. He is especially more aware of his own weakness and mistakes than anyone.

In the same breath, he acknowledges both his strengths and problems as a minister.

I'm aware of my shortcomings. I'm not really a great pastor. I'm more of a soul winner. That's why we've got an older man, a godly minister, to emphasize on the teaching and pastoring part of the ministry. I specialize on reaching people for the Lord.

I believe that soul-winning is still the most important thing for any church. That's my main emphasis; that's also the reason we are not a super-large church. We get them saved, then later on they either move away or go to another church that is more of a teaching church.

Somehow, that soul-winning thrust doesn't seem to be such a weakness. Almost every week, fifteen to twenty souls make public decisions in Evangel Temple. God is directing the activities more than ever, and Jimmy Snow couldn't be happier. That's saying something for a man who bears many scars from past experiences.

The man and the situation is highly reminiscent of another preacher who lived almost two-thousand years ago—Paul. The Apostle's words fit more now than ever.

"God has given me the wonderful privilege of telling everyone about this plan of his; and he has given me his power and special ability to do it well.

Just think! Though I did nothing to deserve it, and though I am the most useless Christian there is, yet I was the one chosen for this special joy of telling the Gentiles the Glad News of the endless treasures available to them in Christ ...

And his reason? To show to all the rulers in heaven how perfectly wise he is when all of his family—Jews and Gentiles alike—are seen to be joined together in his church, in just the way he had always planned it through Jesus Christ our Lord.

Christ has given each of us special abilities—whatever he wants us to have out of his

117

rich storehouse of gifts.

Some of us have been given special ability as apostles; to others he has given the gift by being able to preach well; some have the special ability in winning people to Christ, helping them to trust him as their Savior . . .

Why is it that he give us these special abilities to do certain things best? It is that God's people will be equipped to do better work for him . . . until finally we all believe alike about our salvation and about our Savior, God's Son, and all become full-grown in the Lord—yes, to the point of being filled full with Christ" (Eph. 3:7-8, 10-11; 4:7, 11-13 LB).

There have been numerous thorns among the rosebushes. There have been so many tragedies and triumphs—Nashville, Hollywood, nightclubs, famous friends, salvation beside the mail box, evangelism, the Evangel Temple, divorce, brokenness, victories, a beautiful wife—all have been subliminal parts of Jimmy Snow's unique life. Only when he stands before God in person will the past, present, and future paradoxes be fully understood.

Then, seeing his name etched on Heaven's Book of Life, all of the earthly enigma will be truly worthwhile. Rewards will erase all of the riddles.

But then, God never promised that it would be easy. Jimmy Snow realizes this truth now more than ever, refusing to be beaten by defeats or victories.

Bruised and battered, I can only go forward. A sinner saved by grace. An unworthy servant called to tell others the good news that only Jesus is the way, the truth, and the life. Nothing else comes close. I cannot go back. I cannot quit.

NOTE: Some quotes and paraphrased portions are taken from the book *I Cannot Go Back*, written by Jimmy Snow with Jim and Marti Hefley, Copyrighted © 1977 by Logos International, used by permission from the author and publisher.

DONNA STONEMAN—FREE FROM THE BURDEN

Former dancin', mandolin pickin' centerstager of the award-winning Stonemans

It's just an impromptu jam session in a Nashville apartment, but the room resounds as Donna Stoneman's frisky mandolin and a visitor's mellow guitar blend with happy voices.

Seems my life was just a waste of time,
And if ever a soul was useless—it was mine;
But somehow in my darkness I asked God to give me
    light—
Now I've found a meaning and I know it's right.

With guitar in hand I've taken to the road;
I'm free from the burden of my load.
"So you're into Jesus"—that's what they say to me,
But I answer, "No. Jesus is into me!"

Because I've learned that peace will come
If we only let it.
The goal is not to keep the faith
But to learn to spread it;
So with a smiling face and a loving heart—
I know these words are true:
Don't get into Jesus, but let Jesus get into you.*

Donna Stoneman is so excited about being a Christian that it's contagious. Singing is just an avenue for the happiness bubbling inside to be released. As she travels to schools, colleges, and churches singing, the beautiful fabric of her life continues to be woven together by the Master Weaver.

What a difference. Just a few years ago, her life was a tattered fragment. On the surface, Donna was a member of one of America's premier singing groups. On the inside—that was a different story.

Donna was one of twenty-three children that her mother carried. Of those, fifteen babies were full-term. "Only" thirteen grew to adulthood. Pop (Ernest V.) Stoneman grew up near the mining community of Iron Ridge in Carroll County, Virginia. He met his future wife, Hattie Frost, in nearby Galax, Virginia. While eeking out a painfully poor living as a carpenter in Bluefield, West Virginia, he decided to get into show business. This decision eventually moved the young family to Carmody Hills, Maryland.

Under the direction of Ralph S. Peer (who later discovered the legendary Jimmie Rodgers and the Carter Family), in

1924, Ernest V. Stoneman became the first country artist in history to cut a record. That original disc, "The Sinking of the Titanic," which Pop also wrote, the flip side was "The Face That Never Returned"—eventually sold over a million copies in a three-year period.

The demand for his records quickly spiraled so much that at one time he recorded under eighteen different names, such as Alex Gordon, Uncle Bud Hawkins, and for eight different labels. It was obviously before legal restrictions were imposed on the infantile recording industry.

Sudden prosperity and popularity blossomed on the historic singer. His contribution to country music was enormous, though he continues to be overlooked by the Country Music Hall of Fame. He did numerous recordings and performances during the twenties; in 1929, the world crashed in.

The developing recording industry shut down. Everyone seemed to be out of work, regardless of occupational background. There were few jobs available anywhere. Pop tried to get back into carpentry but no jobs were open. He began building a house since the family couldn't pay the rent to live in others' homes. Unfortunately, money and supplies ran out before a roof could be added. There were no more materials to be scrounged, so for several years the "roof" was huge surplus canvas slung over the timbers.

When the Depression started, Dad lost a lot. The family was helped sometimes by the Salvation Army. One thing that helped was my parents' belief that God would provide. God did bring them through; they didn't starve to death, even though Pattie (Donna's sister) fainted from hunger one day at school. I came along after the Depression.

Although money was scarce, music brought help and happiness through the darkest hours. Dad Stoneman had an unusual way to teach the children how to play the instruments that he and Mom had accumulated.

He used the best reverse child psychology. He and Mommy

played the different musical instruments, then he would leave a fiddle or guitar or banjo on a bed, telling us kids to "leave it alone."

Of course, as soon as he left the house, we couldn't resist picking up and playing the instruments.

In turn, each youngster from the oldest to the youngest member eventually learned to play. The next step was breaking into the family picking sessions.

I remember the first time I ever played with the family. The rest of the older brothers and sisters were there. I was very young but I had been practicing by myself. As they played together, I got the mandolin and started strumming along. I finally looked at Daddy and he grinned so big.

Each kid came into the musical fold that way, making their debut in the living room or out on the front porch. As the Stonemans played for more and more dances and parties in the Washington, D.C., area, the younger performers learned to play on stage. Donna was only eight when she started appearing regularly.

As the family's popularity grew during the forties and fifties, so the group moved from dances and talent contests to concerts and television appearances.

We were on television before I had even seen one. A man named Connie B. Gay had a show in the D.C. area called "Gaytime"; he had a lot of the Nashville-type acts. We won a contest and got to be on it—a bunch of hillbillies. The boys had plaid shirts with handkerchiefs around their necks; the girls had dresses made from flour sacks.

At this time we were just kids. I used to sing along and play the mandolin. When I sang off-key, I would always make faces. I didn't know it, but when we were on television that first time, I made a face and they pushed the camera right up to my face for the audience to see. A girl friend told me about it later.

The little blonde girl who made faces and danced around the stage playing her mandolin became one of the trademarks of the versatile, crowd-pleasing family. Their career not only flourished, but individual members began to create an impact on the music industry. Scotty Stoneman, for example, was to win the National Fiddle Championship nine years in a row. Donna was later to be called the best mandolin player in the world by Jethro Burns (Homer and Jethro) on the Mike Douglas Show. Roni Stoneman was to become a household hero for her famous portrayal of the nagging housewife on TV's "Hee Haw." The Stonemans together were to become one of the country's hottest groups.

Though all of this prestige was in the uncertain, unknown future, already drastic changes had begun in Donna's young life—changes that were to affect her for years to come.

As a child, since we were so poor, I was made fun of, even beat up. When we got on TV that first time, though, I suddenly became popular at school. Pride really set in on me. I would tell the kids at school, "I don't remember you."

In the next twenty years she was a member of one of America's truly great country acts. She and her talented family were an exciting "show" group, almost always stealing the scene from other famous artists that they performed with. Through it all, Donna experienced many of the repercussions often associated with stardom.

I felt so lonely; I felt alone even with my family. People saw me dancing from one end of the stage to the other looking very happy. They said that I had an angelic appearance, but that was on stage. On and off, my pride mounted. In my heart, I was condemning other stars. I prided myself on being morally good—never cursed or drank—so I figured God must be lucky to have somebody like me. That attitude is the most deadly of all sins because a humble heart is the only one He'll listen to.

Pride was understandable as the group continued to see growing success. Later, during the 1950s, Jack Clement began working with the Stonemans as songwriter, record producer, co-manager, adviser, and friend. In 1956, the family won the "Arthur Godfrey Show" two straight weeks, then later came back to do the "Arthur Godfrey and Friends" program. Also in 1956, an unusual circumstance gave the family an additional financial boost. Pop Stoneman won a contest on "The Big Surprise"—a television quiz program. The prize was a whopping $20,000. Suddenly, he and his brood became full-time performers.

In the late fifties, there were three Stoneman groups playing different styles of music. Washington, D. C., Virginia, and Maryland were covered with the versatility of these multi-talented performers.

After establishing their musicianship in the Capitol area, they left to work from a new base, Los Angeles, in 1964. The timing was perfect for their bluegrass-turned-to-folk style. Young people were beginning to turn onto the Joan Baez-Peter, Paul, and Mary sounds. The Stonemans were giant successes at the Monterey Folk Festival, Disneyland, and on nationally televised shows—"Hollywood Palace, "Shindig," the "Steve Allen Show," the "Jimmy Dean Show," the "Meredith Wilson Special," and "Danny Thomas' Special." They appeared with such notables as Debbie Reynolds and Andy Griffith.

After doing the whole California scene—from folk to "hippie"—they moved to Nashville. Jack Clement had previously transferred his talents there. In Tennessee, they were featured on a regular syndicated television show, "Those Stonemans," which was broadcast regularly coast-to-coast for several years. In addition to the demanding television and recording sessions, they kept a rough and exhausting travel schedule that kept them away from home up to eighty-five percent of the time.

During 1966, the group reached another pinnacle by being voted the Country Music Association Vocal Group of the Year. "Five Little Johnson Girls" became one of the country's top-rated songs.

Their showmanship emblazoned millions of television

screens as they appeared on the major network shows—"Johnny Carson's Tonight Show," "Glen Campbell's Show," Johnny Cash's program.

They won another CMA award in 1970, but their appearances were hardly limited to "country" places. The Stonemans played to enthusiastic audiences on a variety of lavish stages—The Fillmore West in San Francisco, the London Palladium, the Las Vegas Landmark Hotel.

They recorded for RCA and MGM. "Christopher Robin" and "Tupelo County" both hit the legendary number one rating in some places of the nation. "Who'll Stop The Rain" and "Proud To Be Together" (written by Cathy Manzer) also hit many charts.

Cathy Manzer, a songwriter friend, remembers the excitement this group caused:

They were an unbelievable show group. Each one in the group seemed so genuinely talented. When they got into their act and started playing, they completely "knocked out" everybody. Nobody could follow them, not even the biggest performers.

As the group continued to ride fame's crest, tragedy started striking. Pop Stoneman died on Friday, June 14, 1968, after a lengthy illness. His family experienced another blow by losing their World Champion Fiddler brother, Scotty, two years later. Half a decade later, Mom Stoneman joined her husband and children. In the meantime, though the family became a top-rated group, Donna sank lower in her varied problems, much lower than her stage grin showed.

My marriage was on the rocks. The problems got so bad that I thought "I can't live this way any longer." I wasn't happy. There wasn't any purpose in my being here. I even contemplated suicide, but I had heard that killing yourself was an unforgivable sin.

I was morally good, so I accused God for all the problems. I had everything materially that I wanted, but the more I earned, the more unhappy I became.

By the early seventies, Donna's marriage had ended in divorce, and her reason for living seemed even more obscure.

I had run away from God, turned away from Him, but in 1972, after the most agonizing six or seven months of bitterness and unhappiness, I told the Lord—"If You want me, here I am." Up until then I had known about Jesus, but I didn't know why He had died on the cross. I accepted Him and found that He had died to take away my pride and give **real** *riches that I had sought all my life.*

As with so many young Christians who have made the initial step of giving their hearts to Jesus, Satan stepped in with his cruel collection of question marks.

I had finally given my life to Christ, but I didn't know what to do. I was sick of music. I was sick of life. My marriage hadn't worked out. I started attending a church after I became a Christian, but they just showed spiritual food, without telling how to get it.

Finally, the gentle hand of Jesus began to nudge me. His silent voice said, "Leave it all behind, and I'll give you a peace and security you've never had. I'll show you real life."

Up until then, my one confidence was in my music and career, so it took me awhile to leave. I didn't want to turn my back on all I had worked for, but I kept hearing the peaceful, gentle Voice. When I did leave, the chain was broken. The pride wasn't gone but it was defeated.

I began to get into the Bible, but I was confused. I prayed, "Please lead me to a pastor who will teach me about You."

Donna was led to the Lord's Chapel, church home of several other Nashville personalities. Though the pastor, Brother Moore, was a fan of the Stonemans, he didn't feed her pride by asking her to testify or by mentioning that she was there.

I really didn't want to go there because I knew that he'd have me get up and talk, but when I went, he didn't ask me to. I didn't want to go up and witness, but I wanted attention. I said to myself, "Here I am in the audience, and he hasn't even said anything about me." My ego was hurt. I decided to never go back, but the Lord continued to lead me back there.

Through Brother Moore I began to see that "we can do no good in ourselves." Anything that is good is through Jesus Christ. He also told us that in our spiritual combat, **we** *were our own biggest problem.*

Just as Jesus really began to defeat her pride, Satan flashed glittering dollar signs in front of her eyes.

When I stopped working with the family, money became scarce. Everyone said "Donna is off the track." Like the children of Israel in the wilderness, I started believing that maybe it was better in the world. I thought about going back, but the Lord spoke to me—"Trust Me."

It was a problem because the devil came as an angel of light. I began thinking that I'd do God more good to return to the group where I could work **and** *testify for Him. The Lord showed me the verse, "No man, having put his hand to the plow and looking back is fit for the kingdom of God."*

Not only was money and work a good reason for her returning to the group, but there was a deep loyalty to her brothers and sisters whom she had worked with for so many years.

That was one of my biggest fears. After losing Dad, Scott, and Roni to "Hee Haw" and the movies and the Dixie Dance Kings, it seemed close to impossible for them to continue as a group. I was the last to leave. I didn't want to see them lose it all. I asked God for a miracle (as I'm sure they did), and He worked it out.

Van, Jimmy, and Patsy are still active as the Stonemans. They also have two other talented members working with them who are not Stonemans. The group is still very great, playing all over, getting standing ovations nearly every show.

God blessed me by continuing to answer. I praised Him for the answers and He confirmed it by supplying my needs. He always does, you know.

God not only patiently nurtured the growth of His new child, but He also began opening a new career. It was with the same mandolin and smile but this time with a different, new song.

During 1977, God led Donna Stoneman and Cathy Manzer (who had traveled for awhile with the Stonemans) together again. Not only was it God's direction for these two new Christians to help each other grow spiritually, but it was the beginning of a new musical purpose. Donna's mandolin-mastery and Cathy's writing, and guitar strumming, form the musical basis for a music ministry that spread from a share-meeting to schools, prisons, hospitals, churches, and colleges. There were tense, difficult moments, but also multitudinous victories.

Soon after starting their ministry together, Donna and Cathy were unknowingly booked into an acid-rock concert at a college in Tennessee. By the time their set came, Donna and Cathy discovered that their audience was "gone" on marijuana and wine. The previous groups had blasted noise to the thousands of drug-dulled ears with gargantuan sound systems and thousands of dollars worth of shiny equipment.

Our two brave souls walked onstage with their comparatively tiny mandolin and guitar. Soon, however, their enthusiasm and talent caught the kids' attention. Apathy turned to admiration. The collegians clapped, yelling for the sound men to "turn 'em up!"

After several songs, Donna flashed her little girl grin. "Now I want to talk to you about Jesus."

Catcalls and distain.

"No, wait a minute. You accepted our talent; now accept what I have to say. I know where you are—I used to search for peace all over, too. After I went through everything else, I found a way—Jesus Christ. Jesus loves you. I love you, too."

From the audience—"No, you don't."

Donna looked out into the sea of unturned faces—"Yes, I do!" The sincerity showed, tension broke, and God began to reach beyond drug-stupors and intellectual hardness.

The same scene has been repeated over and over with different settings and details. Souls have been reached. Lives have been released from the bondage of satanic prisons.

Though they record and travel separately, Donna from a Nashville base; Cathy from her Florida home, money has remained a scarcity—faith a necessity. Donna pensively reflects her new motive for living.

I get the greatest payments when I see people come to Christ. What's even greater, the best is yet to come. I can't wait to see heaven. I'm anxious to see Jesus and my mother and father and Scotty. I want to see all the saints of the Bible, the saints I've helped there, but most of all—Jesus.

In heaven we're going to understand it all. All the bitterness and hassles of this life will be gone and forgotten. Everything will be complete.

New, exciting things are happening everyday for this wandering minstrel. She is surviving because God is sufficient. One unique means of support for her ministry is through Donna's breath-taking artwork (her paintings adorn the walls of some of Nashville's best-known artists and personalities). But mostly, it is through the giving of God's people to His ministry that provides her needs.

Not long ago, Donna Stoneman was a mixture of tattered fragments. Somehow, God cared enough to take the torn pieces laying at the foot of the cross, and He created new woven masterpieces. Instead of brokenness there is beauty; in place of bitterness there is belief; and, instead of bottled torment there is new bubbling happiness.

God has made all the difference for Donna, in this world and in the world to come.

"For we ourselves also were sometimes foolish, disobedient children, deceived, serving different lusts and pleasures, living in malice and envy, hateful, and hating one another. But after that the kindness and love of God our Saviour toward men appeared, not by works of righteousness which we have done, but according to his mercy he saved us, by the washing of regeneration, and renewing of the Holy Spirit; which he shed on us abundantly through Jesus Christ our Saviour; according to the hope of eternal life" (Titus 3:3-7).

With guitar in hand I've taken to the road;
I'm free from the burden of my load.
"So you're into Jesus"—that's what they say to me,
But I answer, "No. Jesus is into me!"

MIKE WARNKE—
FROM SATAN SELLER TO JESUS PERSON

**Satanist high priest who became a top Christian comedian,
recording artist, and best-selling author**

"I can't live in the past."

With a short utterance, Mike Warnke capsulizes his life's philosophy. Though some would like to keep hearing about his past, Mike prefers to be what he calls "a right now, today Jesus person." People like to bring up his past because it was strange and horrible and weird, but until August 22, 1966, there were no tomorrows for Mike Warnke. Little wonder that he wants to forget the past.

Life seemed to squash Mike from the word "go." He is a native of Tennessee, born to alcoholic parents who operated a stereotyped truck-stop. Truck drivers were his friends, baby-sitters, and teachers. Through them he developed not only a colorful vocabulary but also a taste for liquor and small cigars.

When I was still just a kid, I could cuss the wallpaper off the wall! You coulda cut what I said with a butcher knife.

When his parents died, he was taken in by Christian relatives; however, his eleven-year-old foul mouth and their age-old religion beliefs met head-on. After a short stint with his aunts, Mike was taken by the Welfare Department and placed with a foster family in California.

My mother died when I was eight; my dad when I was eleven. They were alcoholic, so I always felt inferior without parents. Others had families but I didn't so I always felt like a freak. What happened to me later is no reflection on the family who took me in. There were no "Hansel and Gretel" stories; I had people who really cared—my aunts in Tennessee did their best, as did my foster family in California. Still, I always felt different and inferior.

I think most orphans feel like this, you know—rejection. As a kid, you feel kinda like your parents ran off and left you or something.

To combat this rejection, Mike began to develop his gift of comical gab.

More than anything, I guess, I used comedy as a defense mechanism—to compensate. To make up for not having a family, I felt like I had to have a lot of friends. I would always try to be the life of the party.

Happiness, contrived or not, is still a life-giving release valve. However, the relief started diminishing as Mike started participating in the occult. Later, in college, as he got deeply involved in doing and pushing drugs, the release valve completely closed.

I was always the comic, but that was lost when I started the dope. Even in high school the joy of life was taken away by a false mysticism.

One reason is that Satan is a complete negative, so Satan worship is completely opposed to any kind of happiness. It's an awful ego trip at first. If you can step on somebody's back to get higher, you just do it. It's a progressive deal that just gets worse and worse. With self-importance so much a part of the whole mentality, I really blew off on an ego trip. As I got more into myself and Satan, the less funny I became.

The Mike Warnke story is well-known with the hundred-thousands of books and records being sold, as well as the hundreds of personal appearances in which he has given his testimony. Still, few know the depth of the inner battles that took place during the period from junior high school until the D-Day in 1966.

Mike experienced an intense desire to scratch his way up the Satanist network. By the time he reached the "top," he had "everything" a nineteen-year-old kid could want. He was a satanist priest with 1,500 worshippers in his coven. He had girls, money, cars, pleasure, adulation—all at the snap of a finger. He directed a large drug traffic. But when the Satanist movement began using him, and when Mike started having overdoses and disease as a result of his own drug habits—then he started a horrible period of disillusionment: of Satan, of his own power, of life, of everything.

I reached the point of dislike for what I was doing, then utter disgust, especially when my friends tried to snuff me out by giving me an OD, my girl friend breaking off the needle in my arm as a parting love gift!

A failure in everything, his life, his purpose, even in suicide attempts, Mike began running. Trying to get away from his past life as well as the ever-present Campus Crusade Jesus people, Mike finally enlisted in the United States Navy.

It was 1966, right in the middle of the Vietnam thing, so just about anybody could get in then if you could just breathe!

There, through the witness of two dedicated Christian roommates, he received the Lord as his personal Saviour in a navy boot camp mop closet. Guess what returned?

The first thing that happened when I got saved—I laughed

my head off. Right there in that mop closet for a long time I just laughed. I was so happy; I felt like I had cheated the devil since he had convinced me that I was forever doomed—could never be saved. When the Lord came into my life, I felt good for the first time in years. Jesus reinstilled my joy instantly.

"Always be full of joy in the Lord; I say it again, rejoice! ... If you do this you will experience God's peace, which is far more wonderful than the human mind can understand. His peace will keep your thoughts and your hearts quiet and at rest as you trust in Christ Jesus" (Phil. 4:4, 7 LB).

I know now that a person cannot face life without a sense of humor. There are too many weird, awful, nasty, yukky, lousy things going on, so if you can't laugh you'll eventually end up in a rubber room counting the buttons on the wall.

"To everything there is a season, and a time to every purpose under heaven ... A time to weep, and a time to laugh" (Eccles. 3:1, 4).

After I got saved I was so happy. I finished my tour of duty as a medical corpsman in Vietnam, then started studying for the ministry, trying to find my place. I tried to be serious and pious. I really tried to fit into the mold of what I thought a Christian should be like, I even attempted to be like other preachers.

I found that the Lord didn't want my imitation of Billy Graham or David Wilkerson. I only had one talent and that was to make people laugh. God wanted to use that talent, not my copy of somebody else.

Laughter and joy had been closeted during the *Satan Seller* era, but God restored the happiness to be conveyed to His people. When that humor was stifled, so was God's blessing on Mike's ministry. Only when it was released could God start using Mike's natural super ability.

At first I would give my testimony, trying to play the whole serious bit. After the service I'd see people coming out;

134

they had the burden, all right, but so much of a burden that they could hardly walk.

So I started interjecting a comical thing here and there. I found that people were more affected by the positive comedy than by the heavy things. A few laughs made it all easier to handle.

I'm a storyteller, not a stand-up comic. I don't use original material that someone sat down and wrote—I use the Bible. True, sometimes any resemblance between my stuff and King James' is purely accidental. My slant is original. I use humor the way Jesus used parables—to communicate His message.

The comedy has not only been used to drive precious truths home to youthful hearts, but it has also been a significant instrument to get rid of the past—both for Mike and for his audiences.

I think that the gift of comedy really took me away from the **Satan Seller** *thing. I mean, being hooked all the time to your past can be a real drag. People have to mature past all that stuff, and it was a blessing of the Lord to be able to start doing the comedy because I could get away from the old satanist priest routine.*

A long time people expected me to be six-foot-seven with forty-four-inch fangs. You know—to arrive at the meeting in a long black car and crawl out of a cofffin and fly in the back door and slide down over the pulpit and say something like (imagine Mike Warnke imitating Vincent Price) "I'm so-o-o gla-a-ad you ca-a-ame toda-a-ay!" You know—like a refugee from an old Gary Paxton record!

That's all behind him now, especially with his "Mike Warnke Alive" and "Jester In The King's Court" albums. Getting rid of the past hasn't always been easy. Mike has even refused large offers for movie rights for the *Satan Seller* and an appearance on NBC's "Tomorrow Show" because of planned emphases on the satanic aspect with little or none of his present Christian life.

The whole process of separating from the old life has

evolved.

I needed this. It's caused a lot of pain and confusion for people to always try to see me as the "former satanist high priest." I praise the Lord for getting me away from it—I'm so glad because I want to talk about the Lord. That's the heaviest one thing that's ever happened to me—accepting Him. You can't live in the past.

God has put His hand of blessing on Mike Warnke's ministry. He is booked constantly in the biggest places: Knott's Berry Farm, Las Vegas, Opryland, Australia, and points between. There have been thousands of success stories.

At the Fishnet '77 in Virginia, Mike finished his set with the 8,000 young people giving a standing ovation. As he left the stage, a mid-teenaged girl met him at the steps and said, "Do you remember me?"

She went on to explain that three years before at another Fishnet she had accepted the Lord when Mike had given an invitation. She had accepted the Lord then walked out into the woods, threw away her dope, and gave Mike the empty stash pack.

I told her that I did remember. She said, "Well, I haven't done any drugs in those three years, all because you showed me Jesus. I've been studying His Word and serving Him, and anytime I get low or depressed, I just take out the cassette tape of your first message when I got saved and remember how much the Lord has done for me."

Life hasn't always been so rewarding or dramatic. There have been problems to counterattack the blessings since that decision in 1966. At first there were death threats by his "old friends" from the California covens.

I just had to claim I John 4:4—"Ye are of God, little children, and have overcome them: because greater is He that is in you, than he that is in the world."

There have been daily problems, too. The devil is always around to hassle any of God's children, especially one who was wrestled so spectacularly from Satan's seemingly secure grip. Sometimes the temptations hit head-on.

Success is one of the worst hurdles in keeping my relationship with the Lord. It's easy to see and believe all the glitter and fame and recognition. I've thought at times that nothing could ever bring me down. That's when I fall down.

I'm not always wise with my blessings, but I do know that the Lord is always there and that He always forgives. He not only forgives my sins, He forgets. If you come back in five minutes and say, "Lord, do You remember that sin I asked You to forgive?" and He says, "Nope!"

It's all so real when Mike Warnke begins speaking. Nancy Honeytree said it best—"He makes you laugh in spite of yourself!" Just Mike's presence on the stage makes God's love even more believable.

He's a master of comedy; perfect in his timing, but beneath the steady stream of one-liners and ridiculous stories, there's a sane, intelligent, loving teacher teaching about real problems that real people face every day. About heavenly promises. About the fruitful Christian walk. His latest album, "Hey, Doc!" and a recent book, are just two more spectacular examples of Mike's ability to communicate to the heart of millions of kids of all ages.

His speech is from the street, but the message is straight from his heart. Kids laugh, then listen because they can vividly see God's truth in action.

I'd like to be remembered for those things—kids who have accepted the Lord, who have gotten off drugs and false trips and gotten into something real, something lasting.

God has changed the unchangeable. Loved the unlovable. And for Mike Warnke, there's no time or reason for looking back at the past.

"See how very much our heavenly Father loves us, for he allows us to be called his children—think of it—and we really *are!* But since most people don't know God, naturally they don't understand that we are his children. Yes, dear friends, we are already God's children, right now, and we can't even imagine what it is going to be like later on. But we do know this, that when he comes, we will be like him, as a result of seeing him as he really is. . . . If we love other Christians, it proves that we have been delivered from hell and given eternal life. But a person who doesn't have love for others is headed for eternal death. We know what real love is from Christ's example in dying for us. And so ought we to lay down our lives for our Christian brothers. . . . Let us stop just *saying* we love people; let us *really* love them, and *show it* by our actions. Then we will know for sure, by our actions, that we are on God's side, and our consciences will be clear, even when we stand before the Lord" (1 John 3:1-3, 14, 16, 18-19 LB).

TEDDY WILBURN—
LOST IT ALL TO FIND EVERYTHING
Younger half of the legendary Grand Ole Opry duo—
the Wilburn Brothers

Photo: Wil-Helm Agency

No one could see behind the glistening smile on the tanned singer in rainbow-splashed Western clothing. Strumming his personalized guitar, Teddy broke into a song with his equally rainbow-splashed brother, Doyle. The Grand Ole Opry audience instantly applauded.

Another smoothly-blended song. Twin guitars twanged. The legendary Wilburn Brothers again slid their close harmony all over the scale in a slow, heartsick winsomeness. Once more, ringing cheers filled auditorium.

Behind the plaudits, behind Teddy's glittering suit and flashing smile—behind it all a deep-down ache was reaching extreme proportions. It was June, 1967. The summer night air seemed to bear down as he walked to his waiting, sleek sedan. Once more, as the applause echoed inside the auditorium, his overpowering problems swept down.

The hectic pace and public appeal demanded more and more from this troubled young performer. 1967 alone was an endless chronicle of close to 250 shows on the road, over twenty Saturday night Grand Ole Opry appearances, involvement in almost 50 recording sessions, work as executive and part-owner with Nashville's Wil-Helm Talent Agency and Sure-Fire Music Publishing Company, hours of writing and rewriting and demo sessions with staff musicians. The problems and pressures of being one of America's leading country singers became overbearing.

It finally got so that I couldn't keep the pace any longer. Doyle was just coming out of a bad marriage, so he wanted to work on the road all the time. That and everything else got to be more than I could take. Finally, I told him—"I quit!!" I said that I would finish the contracts through '67, but that was it. I was through!

Not knowing that ahead were the ultimate depths of despair, drinking, and paranoia—Teddy Wilburn walked out on one of the brightest careers that country music would ever know, a career that had followed a rocky 30-year road starting back in Hardy, Arkansas.

Born November 30, 1931, and named Thurman Theodore, Teddy was the fifth child of Benjamin and Katie Wilburn. Lester Lloyd, Leslie Floyd, Vinita Geraldine, and Virgil Doyle had come into the world several years before to the Depression-ridden farmer and his wife. During the darkest years, Benjamin tried several occupations—trapping, the WPA—in a barely successful attempt to keep food on the hand-hewn table.

As the family faced the final years of the Depression, Benjamin came across something new. One day while taking crossties to sell for twenty-five cents apiece in Hardy, he saw a family playing musical instruments on a street corner.

Speck (known nationwide as Porter Wagoner's sidekick and comedian), Slim, Dusty, and Bea Rhodes had been traveling through Hardy when their car broke down. They were standing on the dusty corner singing, "When You And I Were Young Maggie," trying to collect enough nickels and dimes to fix the already-patched-together auto.

On the way home, Dad Wilburn began to visualize a dream for his children. Within the next few weeks and months, he and Mom taught the children to play musical instruments, and just before Christmas, 1937 (Teddy was a first-grader), the fledging young "Shirt-tailed Children's Band" made its first public appearance.

This less-than-auspicious attempt to put money in their moneyless pocket proved a small but fruitful beginning. With the stairstep children strumming and singing on a Thayer, Missouri, street corner—the "take" of $6.40 began a twelve-year, 300,000-mile trek across the country singing and collecting money whenever possible to pay for groceries and a night's lodging in sometimes buggy tourist cabins.

It used to be a race or a game whenever Dad would get a new shipment of pictures. He'd sit us around a table and have us autograph each copy. We'd try to see who could get finished first so we could go outside and play. Since I was the youngest, just learning to print my name—you know WHO was always last to finish!

In 1938, the young troupe made their first radio broadcast. The Hardy townspeople took up a collection and furnished a panel truck for Pop and the kids to travel to Jonesboro, Arkansas. As they began their program on KBTM with "She'll Be Coming Around The Mountain," Mom sat in Leonard's Cafe back in Hardy with her tears and pride bubbling over. The Wilburns didn't have their own radio so she had caught a ride into town to hear the broadcast.

In 1940, while traveling through Alabama, Dad Wilburn heard that Roy Acuff was having a show and talent contest at the Birmingham Municipal Auditorium, so he pointed the kid-loaded car in that direction. They arrived *after* the talent contest was finished (three flat tires and torrential weather), but the indomitable Wilburn spirit refused to be defeated. He positioned the instrument-laden children at the foot of the backstage steps. When the "King of Country Music" came out after his show, Dad signaled and the kids started singing—"Farther along we'll know all about it . . . "

Roy stood with tears in his eyes watching the five ragamuffins pouring their hearts out. Within weeks, he had them standing on stage spellbinding audiences on the international-broadcast Grand Ole Opry. From the very first Opry appearance, the Wilburn children received 100 pounds of mail. They worked in Nashville capturing America's hearts for six months until the child-labor laws were enforced.

They were the first child act on the Opry, so even after they were forced off the stage, they were already known across the nation. The first big break had happened—they had passed the first giant test. Now they played theaters and clubs and school auditoriums instead of street corners and talent contests.

Soon World War II exploded across the globe. The singing act was broken up by Leslie's being drafted and Geraldine's marriage. Leslie, though wounded in action by a German mortar shell, rejoined the Wilburn Brothers after the war. They soon became regulars on the Louisiana Hayride in Shreveport, Louisiana, until the Korean Confrontation again broke up the group.

After Doyle and Teddy returned from their tours of duty, they formed a duet with Leslie and Lester working as "side men." Their popularity far surpassed prior acclaim, and they worked with the Faron Young Show for almost a year until 1953 when they once again started appearing on the Grand Ole Opry. They've been permanent members since.

In the next twenty-some years, the Wilburn Brothers were to become a legend among legends.

For Decca Records, they recorded hit after hit and numerous

best-selling albums. "Roll Muddy River," "The Knoxville Girl," and "It's Another World" still rank among the biggest country hits of all time. "Trouble's Back In Town" not only remains their audience-appealing theme song, but was voted the Top Country Record in the nation in 1962.

They not only appeared on a Western movie, but were voted the Top Country Vocal Group for five straight years. They won virtually every trade award known to country musicians.

Their "Wilburn Brothers Show," televised for thirteen years is still running into 45 markets, though no shows have been filmed for several years. It featured Loretta Lynn, Harold Morrison, and Don Helms, with the guest list reading like a Country Music "Who's Who."

They proved to be not only superbly-talented, but, also, highly successful businessmen. Their Sure-Fire Music Publishing catalog contains scores of hits—"Fist City," "Fool #1," "Statute Of A Fool," "Wine, Women and Song," "Woman Of The World," "You Ain't Woman Enough," "You're Looking At Country."

Their Wil-Helm Talent Agency booked a gallery of stars: Loretta Lynn (Teddy bought her her first pair of high-heeled shoes), the Osborne Brothers, Sonny James, George Jones, Slim Whitman, Jean Shepherd, Crystal Gayle, Charley Rich, and Stringbean.

Then came June, 1967. The end. Teddy walked out on almost thirty years of show business, an action that was sure to leave emotional scars because it affected so many people.

So many things began happening. Old friendships blew up. Well-known artists walked out of artist/agency contracts. Lawsuits were filed.

I just couldn't cope any longer. The lawsuits were especially hard. So many lies were told in court. I couldn't believe how they got away with it under oath.

Plus, Doyle and I had some encounters. Finally, I told my brothers that I didn't care what happened, I was getting out.

From there, it was all downhill. Looking back now, I realize that God was letting me go through a lot so that I would finally have to turn to Him. If I would only have known what I know now, I would have started searching for answers in the Bible and at church; instead I turned to the bottle. That and my paranoia created problems with every relationship I had—with myself, my family, the artists in Nashvile. It got so that I didn't like anyone.

The downhill tumble continued with another unfortunate experience. Teddy moved to his house in Hollywood, and a Los Angeles dramatics workshop he attended added another link in the enslaving chain.

The approach in method acting is to scrape off any and all inhibitions the student has from performing any and all roles. For instance, I never used foul language much before.

In scraping off what the dramatics coach called "limitations that social standards have created," I became one of the most vulgar-speaking persons ever. Then, when the drinking habit got heavier, the vulgarity increased.

Teddy was arrested once for driving while intoxicated, and his famous name didn't keep him out of jail. As the drinking reached alcoholic porportions, he became so filled with paranoia that he no longer trusted even his family or close friends. Finally, his thoughts turned to suicide.

I had no purpose—no direction. I was so empty. I didn't care for me, so I didn't care for anybody else. Now I know that if you don't even like the man who looks back at you when you shave, that nothing is worth anything. I didn't know that then—no wonder that the reflection wasn't any good; Christ wasn't pleased with what was happening to me.

His was a shattered, scattered life. One of the worst fallacies of our society is that it puts tremendous pressure upon success. The "star" is supposed to make everybody happy—always supposed to keep "happening" and bring in the giant dollars. That pressure has destroyed numerous "stars" as the unnoticing public crushed past. Idol-worshippers have an aversion to "has-beens," so the singing idol—upon reaching the top—must fight for his precarious pinnacle or fall like a crashing avalanche, soon to be forgotten.

Teddy Wilburn knew that constant, persistent pressure. Year after year.

I would go to bed night after night, year after year. I would lie there and wallow in the problems and pressures. I might start twenty or thirty prayers trying to ask for God's help, but I couldn't even finish a prayer—I'd start thinking about my problems. Finally, I'd fall asleep.

Plus, with the drinking, it got even worse. God was convicting me, and conviction either brings victory or frustration. I took the bottle-way out. One of Satan's lies is that he tries to tell you that you can forget your problems and have a good time when you are drinking—that it's the best way to ENJOY life, but it's just a way out—just an escape.

I would wake up so many afternoons and not remember when or how I got home. I gave up trying to remember. This just added to my paranoia.

During the bleak years after the "retirement" in 1967, Teddy also had a bout with hepatitis. By the mid-seventies, he had reached the absolute bottom. Then when there was no way to look but up, God began working dramatically. The months during late 1975 and early 1976 unfolded like a stanza from Larry Gatlin's "Light At The End of Darkness," or Bill and Gloria Gaither's "I Lost It All To Find Everything."

It was because of my own stubbornness that God allowed me to go to such depths. He knew me better than I did—He knew my stubborn personality, and I can now see the reason for it all.

Suddenly, when there were no more answers, the Saviour of the centuries-old Bible stepped into Teddy's troubled life.

His friends began praying for him. As more and more of Teddy's Nashville friends turned to the Lord with their problems, they began joining together in prayer for Teddy. Skeeter Davis got Teddy to go to the Lord's Chapel to a service. Then Mae Boren Axton (an aunt of Oklahoma's former governor) talked Teddy into going to a church service. The deacons of the Lord's Chapel prayed with Teddy.

Though he made no decision that night at the Lord's Chapel prayer meeting, he recognized a new peace; however, that was just the pre-storm calm. Two days later, as he sat drinking his second beer of the morning, he suddenly felt the phantoms of paranoia creeping into his mind. Knowing that he needed help, he called his doctor who told Teddy to come right over. He had barely arrived at the doctor's when a chill hit his body and he started trembling.

The doctor sat dumfounded.

It felt so chilly, and I heard God saying—"I'm preparing you for death!"

I started crying uncontrollably. I said—"I'm going to die tonight!"

God replied, "Oh, no, not tonight; I'm preparing you for when you do die."

I had never heard of anything like this! I asked, "Do You want me to be a preacher?"

"No. I just want you to spread my Word. I will put the words in your mouth."

"What do You want me to do? Do You want me to write religious books?"

God said, "I will help you with your writing."

"Do You want me to write religious songs?"

God repeated, "I will help you with your writing."

I looked at my Jewish doctor friend and said, "I'm being saved!" Then the words started bubbling out. "Listen to me, I'm preaching to you."

He thought I was flipping out, but that feeling that I knew right then was the closest feeling to heaven I'll ever have on earth. The whole experience lasted forty-five minutes or so.

I left the doctor's praising God. I drove down the highway towards home praising the Lord, singing hymns, still crying, when the devil hit me with—"That was me!!"

That stunned me and I began praying "Oh, no. Lord, let me know that it was from You."

I got home and searched through the drawers and closet, finally finding a big, thick Bible in a box. I went to my bedroom and the first thing I opened to was Psalms 60:1-3:

"O God, thou hast cast us off, thou hast scattered us, thou hast been displeased; O turn thyself to us again.

Thou hast made the earth to tremble; thou hast broken it: heal the breaches [brokenness] therof; for it shaketh.

Thou hast shewed thy people hard things: thou hast made us to drink the wine of astonishment."

Those verses made it real. I knew that it was for real and that God had the answers. That night, I accepted the Lord as my Saviour and guide.

I started reading more of the Bible, and for the first time understood it. It was like reading something for the very first time. I said, "Wow! Thank You, Lord."

I got down on my knees and prayed for forgiveness. Then it dawned on me that I should pray and forgive those who had hurt me.

I didn't sleep that night—I just fell deeper and deeper in love with Jesus.

> **"God thirsted for my acknowledgement of Him;**
> **I thirsted but knew not what I was dry for;**
> **I drank and it was so refreshing."***

It was February 19, 1976, a brand-new beginning for a man in Nashville, Tennessee; a time of myriad-voiced rejoicing in heaven.

That was just the start, but the thirst hasn't been quenched. Teddy since has continued getting deeper and deeper into the Bible. Just like Skeeter and Connie and the rest of the Christians in Nashville, Teddy has joined a

---

*Copyright © 1976 by Teddy Wilburn

growing prayer-chain for those who still haven't found the Answer.

Though he has started singing professionally again at the Opry, and though the lines of communication with his brothers have been repaired, his main thrusts are pointed in new and different directions.

He is writing again, this time in a Gospel vein. His first song—"How Did You Take It, Lord Jesus"—was written two days after his salvation experience.

He has become involved with the "Seven Steps" prison program.

For awhile after I accepted the Lord, I was content just to read and study His Word and soak in it at church, but I began seeing the need to get involved in something other than just myself.

The "Seven Steps" program expanded my thinking on the needs of mankind. It really made, for me, something real on the subject "faith without works." When I began working with that group, it made me realize the Christian debt owed to hospitals, elderly people, prison groups, mentally retarded, and so on.

Teddy has begun a new walk, a step that no doubt carries the added pressure of being a new Christian under the scrutiny of an unbelieving public.

People look to performers and any leaders, expecting them to be perfect human beings, but whether that person is a minister, a Billy Graham, or the lowest bum, we need to realize that no other man except Jesus Christ is or ever has been perfect.

He's willing to talk about his past mistakes. It doesn't bother him now, because, as he puts it, "I've found where my perfection lies." As he talks, the "peace that passes all understanding" is evident all over him.

Regardless of what happened yesterday, Teddy Wilburn knows that it's all behind him.

I don't have to live with guilt and hangovers every

morning. I've started once again to enjoy beauty—the outdoors. I've started enjoying life without a glass in my hand.

Regardless of what happens each day, Teddy Wilburn faces each day a new man.

I look back now and realize how good God was to me. We can tear our life and talents down, but God can come and make something beautiful out of our mess.

There is no life torn asunder, totally ripped apart, that God cannot repair and make more beautiful than it ever was before. Praise the Lord!

Regardless what tomorrow holds, Teddy Wilburn knows Who has made the tomorrows possible.

"Blessed be the God and Father of our Lord Jesus Christ, which according to his abundant mercy hath begotten us again unto a lively hope by the resurrection of Jesus Christ from the dead. To an inheritance incorruptible, and undefiled, and that fadeth not away, reserved in heaven for you, who are kept by the power of God through faith unto salvation ready to be revealed in the last time. Wherein ye greatly rejoice, though now for a season, if need be, ye are in heaviness through manifold temptations: that the trial of your faith, being much more precious than of gold that perisheth, though it be tried with fire, might be found unto praise and honour and glory at the appearing of Jesus Christ: whom having not seen, ye love; in whom, though now ye see him not, yet believing, ye rejoice with joy unspeakable and full of glory: receiving the end of your faith, even the salvation of your souls" (1 Pet. 1:3-9).

WES YODER—HE LEADS, I FOLLOW
Top Nashville Christian artist agent

Nashville's booking agencies are unique little civilizations separately clustered throughout Music City. Each has its own "product" to sell; survival depends on superhuman salesmanship. There have been many illustrious talent agents in the colorful history of Music Row: Herbert Long, Jim Denny, Colonel Tom Parker, Jimmy Key, Sol Holliff, Jack McFadden, Larry Loeller, Shorty Lavender, Jack Johnson, Billy Deaton, and others equally well-known.

Today's new breed are a unique conglomeration: some dedicated, others hustling for a piece of the star-studded action; some are professional businessmen, while others are ostentatious clowns. Many adjectives could describe those unique individuals whose lives center around the pushing and scheduling of Nashville's artists.

One special member of this society or agency is a bit unusual. Though he books the brightest rising talents into renowned stages all over the world, he regards it as—get this— a ministry. Is that extraordinary?

His calling to "pastor" his illustrious flock is every bit as urgent and real as are the other priorities in his life. Dharma Artist Agency on the top floor of United Artist Towers is his sanctuary; through it he indirectly ministers to multi-thousands.

It's true that Wes Yoder has an extraordinary calling, but then it's very evident that Wes Yoder is an extraordinary Christian.

He's always been somewhat unusual. He was born in Lancaster, Pennsylvania, into a family with plain-clothes farming and Mennonite traditions. Many of his cousins and his grandparents still belong to the darkly-dressed old order of the Amish.

He was the third of seven children, growing up on a hundred-acre dairy farm. Naturally, as with most rural American families, responsibility came early in life. Chores and fieldwork were an important part of daily life.

His dad had a heart attack when Wes was in junior high school.

Dad could no longer work much, so the responsibility of keeping the farm going fell on the sons, each in turn. It seemed the Lord allowed the spacing of the kids so that each could take the farm for about two years after finishing high school before turning it over to the next brother.

Wes showed early business initiative even in his childish exploits.

I had experience in selling from 'way back. My brothers brought home some Jello to sell to raise money for school equipment. They didn't want to peddle it so I begged my Mother to let me—"I can do it!"—and went around to all the neighbors selling that Jello.

Lots of times Mother and Dad couldn't give us money for

*things. There were instances when it was a big thing for them
to figure out whether they could give us kids even a penny to
buy candy. They were very thrifty, hardworking people, and
when they couldn't give me money I would go out and find
something to sell.*

*I remember one such time when I was in elementary school.
I went to a little private Mennonite school. It seemed that
everyone had a three-speed bicycle but me. I happened to see
one in an American Seed Company magazine; if I could sell so
many packets, I would win a three-speed bike. I don't
remember now whether it was 500 or 1,000 of those seed
packets, but I did it.*

*Mother used to say, "Wes, the Lord owns the cattle on a
thousand hills, but He also needs someone to drive 'em to
market. You're that person. You're going to be a good
businessman someday."*

Perhaps it was self-fulfilling prophecy; perhaps it was a
mother's insight; regardless, her words were correct. She was
right about many other things and influential in the most
important factors of her children's lives, especially
concerning their personal relationship to the Lord.

*I accepted the Lord at thirteen. Our Mennonite pastor
asked a question at the end of one of his messages—"If you
died tonight, where would you go? If you are SURE that you
would go to heaven, raise your hand as a testimony to what
the Lord has done in your heart."*

*Real quick like, I was eliminated. I had never really asked
the Lord into my heart, so I knew where I was headed. I went
home without making any decision at the service. I had a
miserable night.*

*The next morning after tossing and turning all night, I
went in to see my mother. I explained to her about my
problem. Right then she led me to the Lord and prayed with
me.*

Both his business *and* Christian experiences were to be
vital training during the next hectic years.

After eight years at this little two-room schoolhouse, I wanted to go on to Lancaster Mennonite High School where my older brothers had gone.

The law in Pennsylvania provided that children could get a work permit if it was necessary to stay out of school after the eight grade. Because of the financial condition we were in, Dad told me that he was afraid that I as going to have to stay out of school and work.

I asked my parents "If I can raise enough money by myself during the summers, can I go ahead and finish high school?" They agreed, so each Tuesday morning that summer I caught a ride at 3:00 A.M. for Philadelphia (105 miles) to work at the Farmer's Market, hustling for tips by carrying the produce for customers. I'd get home at six each evening.

I made enough to pay my way through school. One summer I also sold enough candy to buy a typewriter to use in my classwork. I guess this background is why I'm always so sensitive to kids going around selling now—I went through it, too.

Wes graduated from Lancaster Mennonite High School, and began his two-year stint on the farm. He had decided to go on to college later but was disillusioned by the general lack of direction of his friends who had gone to college.

They'd come home from Penn State or wherever, and I'd ask them—"What're you gonna do with your life now?" They'd say, "I don't know—get a job, I guess." I finally decided that I'd wait and go to college to study something when I figured out what I wanted to do, rather than merely wasting time and money.

He continued working on the family dairy farm, at the same time building a network of direct sales representatives. By the time he was twenty, he had sixty kids working under him selling cleaning aids.

But, like so many instances in life, talents that he thought he could use exploded in his face.

When I was twenty I had a good moneymaking

153

opportunity. I borrowed $10,000 and made the investment. Well, the main company I was working with went down the tubes. I was stuck high and dry with a $10,000 debt. My dad had co-signed the note since I was still a minor, but he was unable to bail me out.

I went into construction work—a shovel job—for one and half years to try to pay off the bank debt.

Though the re-paying efforts were slightly unsuccessful, Wes did find other outlets for his active energies. He got involved during the construction-working period with an amateur theatre group which staged *Ben Hur*, complete with a gigantic 32-foot ship on the historic stage of the renowned Fulton Opera House in Lancaster.

Then came a 60-voice production of "Tell It Like It Is." Wes and the group scored high marks for their staging success; Ralph Carmichal (the author) came for the premier.

Boosted by the three early achievements, Wes and a friend promoted a Pat Boone comeback-tour show. The place was packed. Pat's agent, obviously impressed, offered Wes an agency position if he would move to California.

Wes jumped at the opportunity, not to join Pat Boone's agency, but to go to Nashville to begin his own. The Boone offer had added fuel to the fire. What he lacked in money or backing, he made up for by sheer nerve and incredible business sense.

When I got here in Nashville, February 27, 1973, I arrived with $27 and a little Gremlin.

A partnership started the new Dharma Artist Agency: Bill Grine (who left in 1974), gospel-rock star Randy Matthews (who left in 1976, taking over the publishing arm of the company), and Wes Yoder. The beginning was less than spectacular. The first office was actually Wes' boarding house bedroom, "complete" with telephone—"Good morning. This is Dharma Artist Agency; Wes Yoder speaking!"

Quickly Wes and his fellow-owners were "welcomed" to Music City, the hard way. A Nashville con man "helped" them get their start by running up some bills in their name and ripping off what little money they had accumulated. It was an expensive lesson. More were to come.

Though the booking end of the business was beginning to pick up, the money part was definitely a problem, especially for Wes who still owed the $10,000 note back in Pennsylvania.

By 1974, I was able to pay only about a thousand off on the loan. Suddenly, I heard the Bible verse which said that we weren't to owe anybody anything, so I came to a decision; I very arrogantly made a "deal" with the Lord—"Lord, I know that it's not Your will for me to be in debt, so I'm not going to tithe anymore until I get the loan paid off. Then I'll give money to You again. Until that time I'll just apply the tithe money to paying it off."

Well, I learned very quickly not to make deals with the Lord, especially on my own terms. In less than a year I doubled my indebtedness. By the end of 1974 I owed $18,000! I was absolutely flipping out.

Not only was the "deal" getting out of control, but other aspects of Wes' life were growing sour. He had gotten out of a regular fellowship with other believers. His spiritual life was taking a slow dead-end drive.

I finally got down and said, "Okay, Lord. What do You want me to do with my life?"

Though the Christian life isn't always storybook perfect, this time things happened. Everything didn't suddenly begin to work out, but for the first time there was hope. All of the problems didn't immediately leave, but as he surrendered more to the Lord, the whole financial picture began to make sense. Nine months later the debt was gone. That was the beginning of changes.

In 1975, the Lord really used my pastor at the First Presbyterian Church, Cortez Cooper. He spoke on Malachi, the third chapter: "Will a man rob God?"

Of course, it seemed ludicrous, but so often we do rob God of what's really His: our money, our time, our life. I had always been manipulative, hoping for things to be given to me. I began to see that I should seek His righteousness first, regardless of what happened, then things would be added. The problem is that the devil is always trying to keep us from seeking the righteousness of God.

Obviously God started adding more "things" as Wes Yoder sought more of the Lord. His business picked up. Dharma is now the exclusive representative for a gospel music "Who's Who": Mike Warnke, the famous standing-room-only Christian comedian, perhaps best-known for his best-selling *Satan Seller* (Logos Books), Myrrh Records, booked all over the world, including Las Vegas, Six Flags, Disneyland, Disneyworld, Knott's Berry Farm, and Opryland; Fireworks, John and Viccijo Witty, Danny Taylor, Scott Wesley Brown, and David Meece (one of the brightest stars on the Christian pop circuit), Amy Grant, and Leon Patillo (former lead singer/keyboard star with Santana).

In an industry often marked with underhanded flashy, "wheeler-dealer" agents—Wes Yoder comes across rather dramatically as a man with a very high calling. At twenty-seven years of age, he stands as a phenomenon on Music Row. Vistors to Nashville's tallest building cannot help being touched by the obvious sincerity and achievement of this young man.

"By the obedience of one, many are made obedient" (Rom. 5:19).

Country, pop, and gospel artists often frequent the UA Towers to talk and share with the warm staff in the Dharma offices.

And, more than anything, God has prepared the exact person to be so instrumental in the exploding Gospel music industry. Somehow the jigsaw pieces all fit together now more than ever before.

It's true that Wes Yoder has an extraordinary ministry, but then, the God he is serving is an extraordinary God.

NASHVILLE SHOWBIZ TRAGEDIES

Nashville is unique in its blends of music, splendor, magnetism, emotions, and people. On the surface, Nashville glitters, beckoning undiscovered stars like a music mecca. Pictures in country music magazines are like cover-to-cover smiles. Success means happiness. Happiness lasts forever. Almost.

New Years Night, 1953. Hank Williams died in the back seat of his Cadillac somewhere between Knoxville, Tennessee, and Oak Hill, West Virginia. During a brief career, Hank became an immortal performer. His legendary songs are still being recorded—"Your Cheating Heart," "Jambalaya," "I'm So Lonesome I Could Die," "Don't Let The Stars Get in Your Eyes," "Take These Chains From My Heart," "I Saw the Light." His was a portrait of contrasts: his childhood in bitter Alabama poverty; his "dues-paying" on the brawling honky-tonk circuit; the bittersweet burst of stardom; the memorable radio broadcasts on the KWKH "Louisiana Hayride," WWVA "Jamboree," and the WSM "Grand Ole Opry," and his losing battles with alcohol, marital problems, loneliness—right up till his death enroute to the concert in Ohio. Only a month before Hank Williams had been fired from the Opry for drunkenness and irresponsibility ("raising hell," they called it). His life was snuffed out in the darkness by a heart attack. For Nashville, country music, and America—it was a tragedy. He was only twenty-nine years old.

Hank Williams was just one in a sporadic line of show business tragedies either directly or indirectly connected with Nashville. Among the happiness, there have always been sad times.

According to recent pop hit, February 29, 1959, was "The Day the Music Died." Nashville was shocked when the report flashed from Clearlake, Iowa. A small aircraft crashed near Clearlake with a pilot and three young singers aboard. All four were fatally injured. Suddenly, Buddy Holly ("Peggy Sue," "That'll Be The Day," "Maybe Baby," "It's So Easy to Fall in Love"), J. P. Richardson—the Big Bopper ("Chantilly Lace"), and Richie Valens ("LaBamba," "Donna") were gone. Buddy was 22, the Bopper 34, and Richie was only 17. What a tragic loss.

On March 6, 1963, Nashville was stunned to hear the latest doomsday news. Patsy Cline ("Walking After Midnight," "I Fall to Pieces"—called the Queen of Country Music), Cowboy Copas ("Filipino Baby," "Hillbilly Heaven"), Hawkshaw Hawkins, and their pilot, Randy Hughes, together had been flying from a benefit concert in Kansas City. They had hit turbulent weather sometime during the night of the Fifth between Dyersburg and Nashville. Early the next morning a fire tower watchman spotted the Piper Comanche. The search crew's worst fears were realized when they saw Hawkshaw's black jacket (emblazoned with the famous Hawk on the back) sticking out of the wreckage.

Less than a year later, "Gentleman" Jim Reeves ("He'll Have to Go") died in another tragic airplane crash. His death certainly wasn't the last. Between 1963 and 1964, eight members of the Grand Ole Opry died in four separate accidents. Since then, Nashville has lost many: Ira Louvin, Stringbean, Tex Ritter, George Morgan, Lefty Frizzell, Jim Denny, Wayne Walker, and so many more.

None of the show business tragedies have stunned Nashville and the world more than the one on August 16, 1977. Suddenly the unbelievable words flashed on millions of television screens: "Elvis Presley is reported dead in Memphis, Tennessee."

Although the news spread quickly around the world, few places were more saddened than Music city. There's a saying in Nashville—"When you cut one of us, we all bleed." Though he was officially from nearby Memphis, many claimed Elvis as one of "us." That day, Nashville ached with one hurt. Even though back during the fifties, Elvis had been told to "go back to driving a truck" by the Opry's Jim Denny, the swivel-hipped crooner had made the Nashville-Memphis "rockabilly" sound not only respectable but profitable. Through the years, Elvis had used Nashville's best musicians, technicians, and back-up singers; Nashville had copied his style and used his influence. For both, the twenty-year-old union had been both profound and long-lasting. It is no wonder then that Music City shed many tears for their friend.

For Hank, Buddy, Patsy, Jim, Elvis, and all the rest, the most amazing aspect of their tragedies was the aftermath. Interspersed among the eulogies, personal "revelations," and exposés, each time the deaths have been marked by the inevitable stories of "deep, personal beliefs in God." Many of these reports have wavered from "fire and brimstone" fatalism to "fleecy-cloud" conjecture.

The truth is, the question of the show business tragedies and each one's eternal destiny was settled before they were taken from us. Their memories and influence will continue to live in the studios and stages of Nashville and beyond, but each one's chance to either accept or reject God's plan of salvation is finished—forever.

The choice—then and now—is this: "There is no eternal doom awaiting those who trust him to save them. But those who don't trust him have already been tried and condemned for not believing in the only son of God" (John 3:18 LB).

As a condemned person, there is *nothing*, fame or money or influence, that can buy one's way out. Fortunately, somebody else paid the debt—Jesus—He was the only one worthy to do so. "For God so loved the world, that he gave his only begotten Son, that whosoever believeth in him should not perish, but have everlasting life" (John 3:16).

Jesus Christ is willing to give that debt-buying gift to anyone who asks: "For the wages of sin is death, but the free gift of God is eternal life through Jesus Christ our Lord" (Rom. 6:23 LB).

Why is this choice so important?

"Except a man be born again, he cannot see the kingdom of God" (John 3:3).

God not only gives the choice and opportunity—"Anyone who calls upon the name of the Lord will be saved [born again]" (Rom. 10:13 LB).

He also gives the power to make that choice and accept Jesus Christ into one's life: "But as many as received him, to them gave he power to become the sons of God, even to them that believe on his name" (John 1:12).

Considering the price (man's nothing for God's eternal everything), the choice shouldn't be too hard to make. "But don't forget this, dear friends, that a day or a thousand years from now is like tomorrow to the Lord. He isn't really being slow about his promised return, even though it sometimes seems that way. But he is waiting, for the good reason that he is not willing that any should perish, and he is giving more time for sinners to repent" (2 Pet. 3:8-9 LB).

There are many who say that Elvis and Hank and Patsy and the rest did know Jesus Christ as personal Saviour. The only thing certain is this—their time to decide is gone forever.

The Nashville people featured in this book, even though time remains for them, have already made the choice and have accepted Jesus Christ into his/her heart.

Considering the eternal consequences, there really shouldn't be any doubt about which way to choose. "For what does a man profit if he gain the whole world and loses or forfeit himself?" (Luke 9:25 RV).

Time will tell the difference.